# NASHVILLE
## STREETS & THEIR STORIES

# NASHVILLE

## STREETS & THEIR STORIES

RIDLEY WILLS II

PLUMBLINE
MEDIA

Printed in the United States of America

Library of Congress Control Number: 2011961335

ISBN: 978-1-937824-01-3

*Front cover photo of Capitol Boulevard courtesy of the Kermit C. Stengel Jr. Collection. Back cover postcards, top: Church Street looking east; middle: Church Street viaduct; bottom: Printer's Alley. Postcards from the collection of Ridley Wills II*

*Cover design by Stoney Noell at EpicLifeCreative.com*

*Page design by Holly Jones*

PLUMBLINE MEDIA, LLC
415 BRIDGE STREET
FRANKLIN, TENNESSEE 37064
615-442-8582
WWW.PLUMBLINEMEDIA.NET

To the memory of my lifelong friend,
Agnes Stokes Fort More,
who died on April 27, 2011.
"Aggie," as she was known to her friends, was interested in nature,
the arts, and her fellow man.
In this book, I write about Riverside Drive,
a "double drive" that went by Fortland,
the handsome farm of Aggie's grandparents,
Louise and Rufus E. Fort, MD.
In 1933, Mrs. Fort beautified the road by planting irises,
Tennessee's state flower,
along its border.
As lovers of the natural world, and its beauty,
this grandmother and granddaughter had much in common.

And

for my friend, Robert L. "Bobby" Reeves,
who suggested that I write this book.

# FOREWORD

In this remarkably thorough compendium of the origins of selected metropolitan Nashville and Davidson County street names, historian Ridley Wills II brings local history literally to the front door of many, if not most, of us who live in Tennessee's historic capital city. If you have ever been curious about the story behind the name of the street, avenue, boulevard, pike, or road where you work or live, you may well find your answer here, as well as a few lesser known anecdotes, in this engaging and interesting book.

In 1784, lawyer and surveyor Thomas Malloy very logically laid out the first plan of the newly incorporated city of Nashville with one-acre squares facing the river and four acres set aside for a public square. According to educator Lizzie Porterfield Elliott's *Early History of Nashville*, "Convenient streets, lanes, and alleys" were to be part of that first plan, and an 1804 map shows the main street to be Market Street. Buildings on the street, the first courthouse, Lardner Clark's store, and the Nashville Inn are long gone, but these earliest streets still exist, and Nashville's public square has remained in the same location for over two centuries.

Established only one year after the end of the Revolutionary War, Nashville's street names reflect both local and national history and sometimes even the topography. Some of the earliest street names indicate where the street led or how it functioned, but they also recall street names common in other American cities of the same period, such as Philadelphia, Boston, and Baltimore. As Nashville grew and neighborhoods developed south to Rutledge Hill, north to Germantown, east to Edgefield, and west to West End, smaller roads took the names of local residents. Longer pikes, extending like the spokes of a wheel from the hub of the city center to outlying communities, took the names of their destinations: Charlotte, Whites Creek, Franklin, Murfreesboro, Gallatin, Hermitage, and Nolensville.

The street names in this book point to the stories of particular people who have lived in this place as well as their homes, institutions, and even relationships. Old Hickory, Acklen, Belle Meade, and Granny White may be well-known names to anyone familiar with local history. Less so are names like Blue Hole Road, Bontemps, Enquirer, Clendenin, or Shute Lane. In some cases, Nashvillians have also honored national figures such as presidents and military heroes, and even the Marquis de Lafayette (except that we use our own Nashville pronunciation).

Unfortunately but perhaps necessarily, a controversial city ordinance followed other cities around the country and changed the names of streets running north and south, west of the Cumberland River, to numbers in 1904, making it easier to navigate a growing metropolis. Both history and a little poetry were lost in the process. Local groups fought the change unsuccessfully, as the author will tell you. But fortunately, he includes and explains many of these first street names in this collection. After you have heard College, Cherry, Summer, and Vine, it will be difficult to think of Third, Fourth, Fifth, and Seventh Avenues in the same way again.

In short, this book will serve as a handy reference for historians, history buffs, and anyone who is curious about names, stories, and the most particular and often hidden history of a community. Some street names will be answers in themselves. Others may well lead you, like they did me, to want to dig deeper into the stories of the people who shaped our neighborhoods and our city. This book will be your key to those stories and to an additional appreciation of Nashville's past. I recommend that you keep Ridley Wills' book on the library shelf or even in the glove compartment at all times.

Ophelia Thompson Paine

# PREFACE
# AND
# ACKNOWLEDGMENTS

On April 1, 2011, my friend Robert L. "Bobby" Reeves suggested that I write a book about Nashville streets. His thought was that many Nashvillians, particularly newcomers, have no idea whom many of our streets were named for or when they were built. Bobby's idea struck a chord with me because, having recently turned in a manuscript to potential publishers on a history of the YMCA of Middle Tennessee, I was looking for another writing project. I had in mind several alternatives, but none of them really screamed, "Yes, that's it!"

The idea of telling stories about Nashville's streets was very appealing, so I immediately started keying into my laptop stories about Granny White Pike, Harding Pike, White Bridge Road, and other streets I have been familiar with all my life. By early May, I found that I had keyed material on nearly five hundred streets in my computer. I've never written a manuscript that fast. One reason that this came so easily is that I live only five minutes away from the Metropolitan Archives in Green Hills. This valuable facility is a treasure trove of information for any researcher of local history. There, almost within arm's reach, are maps, subdivision plats, newspaper articles on streets, and local histories of many communities in Davidson County.

I am particularly grateful that Bobby Reeves gave me the idea of writing this book. It has been great fun, and I have learned a lot.

Equally important, Ken Feith, the director, and his able and knowledgeable assistant, Debbie Cox, have been most helpful. Debbie must have spent five hours researching a single street, Riverside Drive. Also at the archives on a regular basis is Paul Clements, a longtime friend and fellow local historian, whose knowledge of early Nashville history is unparalleled. Both he and Debbie read my manuscript and offered corrections and wise suggestions.

Ophelia Paine, another longtime friend, and a sixth-generation Nashvillian, agreed to write the preface. I must say Ophelia was a perfect choice as, despite her unassuming nature, she is extremely knowledgeable on local history, having served on the staff of the Metropolitan Historical Commission from 1986 to 1998, and now serving on the Tennessee Historical Commission board. With help from folks like Ophelia, who also edited my manuscript, this book is much more complete than it would otherwise have been.

Others who contributed were Linda Winn, a friend on the staff of the Tennessee Historical Commission, and Beth Odle, of the Nashville Public Library. Linda knew the names of a sizeable number of Nashville streets named for prominent African Americans. I simply would have missed a number of these had she not helped me. Beth knows more about old Nashville photographs than anyone in town. She had previously been a great help in finding wonderful photographs for my book, *The Hermitage At One Hundred: Nashville's First Million-Dollar Hotel*, published in 2009. She graciously found several of the really great photos of Nashville's streets of the past for this book.

Some others who have contributed are Bill Akers, Tom Byl, Linda Center, William G. "Bill" Coble Jr., Donya Downey, David Ewing, Karl Haury, Jim Hoobler, Charles "Chuck" Johnston, Elizabeth McLaurin, Ann Parsons, Bruce P'Pool, MD, Vi and Don Prosser, John Tilford, Dudley Warner II, and Ridley Wills III. I appreciate your help.

I also want to thank Andrew Miller and Holly Jones at Plumbline Media, along with Tammy Spurlock, for their help in the editing, design, and layout of this book. Thanks to Stoney Noell of Epic Life Creative for his cover design.

One of the many ways Paul Clements helped me was to scan his files on Nashville newspapers and tell me when and which newspapers had stories on Nashville streets. From looking at these articles on microfilm at the Tennessee State Library and Archives, I discovered how contentious the fight to simplify street names was and how long the controversy lasted. The change came when a sub-committee of the city council, consisting of P. M. Estes, Dr. W. W. Green, and Ed M. Wrenne, recommended to the council that the names of the first thirty streets running north and south, west of the Cumberland River, be given numerical names of First Avenue through Thirtieth Avenue, respectively. At a council meeting on November 10, 1904, this recommendation, slightly amended, was approved.

This change didn't just come up in 1904; it had been argued about at least as far back as 1885, when the Board of Public Works recommended that the streets downtown, running north and south, be changed to the "more progressive" First Street through Ninth Street.[1] The idea got nowhere in the 1880s. As one gentleman wrote on February 7, 1886, "There's no hope for a change to be actually affected for many years at best. Nashville people have spent most of their lives learning the old names and will not take kindly to the new."[2] He was correct. When the change was pushed through by the city council eighteen years later, it was done despite the vociferous opposition of many individuals and groups, including the Centennial Club.

Those in opposition didn't give up easily. In the winter of 1908–09, the Review Club, a group of prominent Nashville women, asked that action be taken to have the names of the downtown streets restored to the "old, historic names."[3] They had plenty of support, including that of financier James E. Caldwell; attorney Morton B. Howell; ex-governor James D. Porter; Dr. William Anderson, pastor of the prestigious First Presbyterian Church; Bishop Oscar Fitzgerald of the Methodist Episcopal Church South; and Ira Landrith, president of Belmont College.

On April 22, 1909, Councilman Marlin introduced a bill in the city council to restore the old names. His bill was defeated 16 to 9. Councilman Marlin, whom the *Nashville American* called "Paul Jones Marlin," announced that the fight had just begun and that he would introduce a similar measure at the next meeting of the council.[4] Despite his bravado, the repeal effort lost steam and the losing side reluctantly gave up the fight.

I make several references to macadamized streets built by the Belmont Land Company, Bransford Realty Company, Foster & Creighton, the Inglewood Land Company, and others in the late 1800s and early 1900s. Wilbur Foster Creighton explained the process in his biography of his father, *Life Story of Robert Thomas Creighton*, published in 1967. I think it might be helpful to use Creighton's own words to describe how the paving process worked:

Streets were then built according to the methods originated by John L. McAdam, 1756–1838, a Scotsman. The bedding stone was about 8" thick. It was placed by hand on the smoothly graded ground. The parts higher than 8" were then "knapped" or broken by hand to 8". The pieces broken off filled the void in the base. On this was placed stone about the size of a fist, four inches thick. This layer was compacted by large rollers pulled by mules. This was wetted and rolled until the surface was smooth.[5]

Traffic on streets such as Greenwood and Patterson also helped press down the stones. However, on the edges of the streets, where traffic was light, loose pieces could be found by neighborhood boys who used them to settle personal differences. Fortunately, Nashville streets are paved with asphalt these days, providing a smooth surface and fewer opportunities for boys to collect ammunition.

Enjoy the book and the illustrations.

Ridley Wills II
June 7, 2011

# NASHVILLE

## STREETS & THEIR STORIES

**ABBOTT MARTIN ROAD** extends east from Lynnwood to Hillsboro Pike. A plat of the subdivision plan for property owned by Mrs. Mary Billington in June 1926 showed present-day Abbott Martin as Abbott Road, named for an Abbott family who lived there in 1919. Twenty years later, a city map showed the name of the street to be Abbott Martin. The name "Martin" was added in honor of Alex Martin, who lived on the road. Many Nashvillians with Sewanee, Tennessee, ties think the road was named for Abbott Cotton "Abbo" Martin (1901–76), an eccentric University of the South professor who taught English and French literature from 1928 until 1969. Born in Ackworth, Georgia, in 1901, Abbo was likely a graduate student at the University of Mississippi when Abbott Road had already been built. When asked by Nashville students whether Abbott Martin Road was named for him, Abbo was usually noncommittal.

**ACADEMY PLACE**, in 1898, ran from Fillmore Street across Lindsley Avenue to Carroll Street (formerly Asylum Street). It was named for Montgomery Bell Academy, which occupied the entire city block bounded by Kuhn Street, Academy Place, Lindsley Avenue, and University Street from 1881 until the school moved in 1913. Today, Academy Place runs from Hermitage Avenue to Lindsley Avenue in a landscape vastly changed.

**ACKLEN AVENUE** runs across the side of Love Circle from Orleans Drive to Twenty-First Avenue South. The name honors the prominent Joseph Acklen family. (Acklen Park Drive is also named for this family.) The oldest house on Acklen Avenue is located at 2134. Built in the 1870s, it was originally the home of Col. John C. Burch, who became secretary of the United States Senate in 1879. In about 1900, James C. Bradford, president of the Belmont Land Company, gave the old Belmont mansion gateposts at the corner of Hillsboro Pike and Acklen Avenue to Walter Stokes, who installed them on the entrance to his home, Breezemont, just over one mile south on Hillsboro Pike. Before 1930, parts of Acklen Avenue were named Dodd and Marshall.

**ACKLEN PARK DRIVE** begins at Murphy Road and runs northeast before turning southeast to end at West End Avenue. *See Acklen Avenue.*

**ADELICIA AVENUE**, which runs from Nineteenth Avenue South to Twentieth Avenue South, was named for Adelicia Acklen, the daughter of Joseph Acklen,

*This 1967 aerial view of Green Hills shows, near the lower right corner, eight undeveloped acres on Hillsboro Circle that H. G. Hill Jr. gave the Metropolitan Nashville YMCA that December as the site for the Southwest Family Branch. To the left is Abbott Martin Road and, beyond it, the Green Hills Shopping Center where Cain-Sloan's first suburban store, which opened on October 25, 1965, is visible.*

YMCA OF MIDDLE TENNESSEE COLLECTION

who lived at nearby Belmont Mansion. Earlier, Adelicia Avenue had been named Dodd Avenue.

**ADLAI STREET**, off Whites Creek Pike beyond West Trinity Lane, was named for Adlai Stevenson, vice president of the United States under the Grover Cleveland administration.

**ALAMO PLACE**, in West Nashville, is adjacent to Charlotte Park. It was likely named for the Alamo in San Antonio, Texas, where approximately 180 to 258 Texans were killed by Mexican Gen. Antonio de Santa Anna's forces on March 6, 1836, after a thirteen-day siege of the Alamo Mission. Many Tennessee volunteers were also killed, including David Crockett. The number of Mexicans killed or wounded was estimated at between 400 and 600.

**ALLENDALE DRIVE** is a short street between Old Harding Pike and Keyway Drive in West Meade. It was named for Mrs. Neil Cargile's family, who built a house nearby. Her maiden name was Eleanora Sedberry Allen.

**ALTA LOMA ROAD** is in Goodlettsville, adjacent to Rivergate Square. The word means "high ground." It was subdivided by Bransford Realty Company in 1913.

**ANTIOCH PIKE** runs along Mill Creek in Southeast Davidson County. When opened in 1846, the pike was known as Mill Creek Valley Pike. An Antioch historian, Herschel Lane, said that the small village of Antioch and Antioch Pike were named for the Antioch Baptist Church, organized in 1810. Antioch Pike and the other turnpikes in Davidson County were privately chartered from the county to individuals or groups of individuals. The charters required that they build, operate, and maintain a good road sixteen feet wide. The county also dictated the amount of toll the owners could charge for its use.

**THE ARCADE**, located between Fourth and Fifth Avenues, is an enclosed pedestrian street. It is 360 feet long, about 75 feet wide, and features a gabled glass roof. Daniel Buntin, a Nashvillian, was inspired to build it by visiting similar malls in Europe. More than forty thousand people were said to have visited the Arcade on opening day, May 20, 1903. The Arcade is owned today by a private corporation that has controlled it for many decades.

**ASHWOOD AVENUE** first appeared in the city directory in 1908. It was not until 1923 that residential development began in this area. That year, twenty lots on both sides of the street west of Hillsboro Pike were advertised for sale as the Hillsboro Heights subdivision. The street runs east from Natchez Trace to Twelfth Avenue South.

**ASYLUM STREET**, on Rutledge Hill, was named for the Tennessee School for the Blind that faced Fillmore Street just beyond the city hospital. The street and the school are no longer there. *See Carroll Street.*

**BAILEY STREET**, behind Miller's Clinic in East Nashville on the west side of Gallatin Pike, was named for D. H. Bailey, whose home faced Gallatin Pike. A subdivision plan for his property was filed on June 11, 1914. Today, Bailey Street

*The Arcade, which opened on May 20, 1903, is shown here a few years later. The American flags and balloons, suspended from the gabled glass roof, added to its attractiveness.*

RIDLEY WILLS II COLLECTION

runs north in broken segments from West Eastland Avenue to beyond West Greenwood Avenue.

BALDWIN COURT runs south off Rowan Drive in a subdivision west of Whites Creek Pike. The street was named for James Baldwin (1924–87), African American essayist, novelist, playwright, poet, and civil rights advocate.

BANK STREET, between First Avenue and Second Avenue North in downtown Nashville, was named for the nearby banks. The street's earlier name was Clark Alley. The street no longer exists.

BAPTIST WORLD CENTER DRIVE connects Whites Creek Pike with Brick Church Pike. The street was named for American Baptist College, located at 1800 on this street. The college opened its doors for the training of Christian workers on September 14, 1924, under the name of the American Baptist Theological Seminary. The college is best known for having educated civil rights champions including Julius Scruggs, Bernard Lafayette, Jim Bevels, William Barbee, and John Lewis. These young men were all heavily involved in the Nashville student sit-in movement for justice and change between February 13 and May 10, 1960. The students sat at segregated lunch counters, marched, and persevered through arrests and beatings before they achieved victory in beginning the desegregation of Nashville's public facilities. Today, the school continues its commitment to educate students to go into the world "to do justice, to love mercy, and to walk humbly before God."[6]

**BARTON AVENUE** first appeared in the city directory in 1912, with one resident. The street is located on land that was earlier part of the Glen Oak estate. Episcopal minister Charles Tomes purchased fifteen acres between Hillsboro and the Old Natchez Trace in 1854 and built Glen Oak, that still stands at 2012 Twenty-Fifth Avenue South. In 1912, Bransford Realty Company subdivided the Glen Oak property that had been expanded by a subsequent owner, Edgar Jones. The subdivision extended from Long Avenue (renamed Blair Boulevard) on the south to Jones Avenue (renamed Fairfax Avenue) on the north, and included Essex and Barton Avenues.

**BATAVIA STREET** is between Twenty-Second Avenue North and Twenty-Seventh Avenue North. Another section runs from Twenty-Eighth Avenue North to Thirty-Ninth Avenue North. The street's name comes from the land occupied by Batavians during the Roman Empire. Today, that land is part of the Netherlands. Batavia Street was formerly known as Zollicoffer Street, named for Felix Zollicoffer, a Tennessee congressman turned Confederate general, who was killed at the Battle of Fishing Creek on January 19, 1862.

**BATTERY LANE** is the section of Harding Place between Granny White Pike on the west and Franklin Pike on the east. Battery Lane formed the northern and eastern boundaries of the Overton Lea estate. The lane was named for the artillery pieces positioned near there during the Battle of Nashville fought on December 15–16, 1864. According to Robert Neil, an early resident, in 1923 the lane was little more than a bicycle path so narrow that two cars couldn't pass.

**BATTLEFIELD DRIVE** runs from Franklin Road to Belmont Boulevard. It was named for the December 1864 Battle of Nashville. A Battle of Nashville monument, originally on Franklin Pike, now stands near the intersection of Battlefield Drive and Granny White Pike.

**BAXTER STREET** runs parallel to Gallatin Pike between Hart Lane and McIver Street. It was named for Jere Baxter.

**BEAR ROAD**, in Woodmont Estates, connects the loop in Valley Brook Road. The street was built in 1937 as part of the subdivision of the G. A. Puryear estate. Mr. Puryear gave it that name because he used to admonish children to watch out for bears when they played in the woods behind his house on Hillsboro Pike.

**BEAUREGARD DRIVE**, in Forest Hills, south of Tyne Boulevard, was named for Confederate Gen. Pierre Gustave Toutant Beauregard by developers Karl Haury and Reese Smith Jr. in the 1960s.

**BELL ROAD** is a five-lane thoroughfare that runs from Tusculum to the Una area in Southeast Davidson County. The road was named for the family of Benjamin Bell, who bought three hundred acres between Hamilton Creek and Stones River in 1822. The Bell family cemetery was near the road.

**BELL STREET** ran from Sixth to Eighth Avenues South and was named for John Bell, who at age thirty-seven, was elected speaker of the United States House of Representatives. In 1841, he became secretary of war. Bell next served as a U.S. senator and ran for president of the United States in 1860. Today, a convention center covers what once was Bell Street.

**BELLE MEADE BOULEVARD** is a three-mile-long divided boulevard that leads from Harding Pike to Page Road. The contract for its construction was let in August 1910. Four years later, the boulevard, which had been completed to Harding Place, was extended along the southern edge of the Nashville Golf and Country Club across Richland Creek to the present entrance of Percy Warner Park. Luke Lea built the divided boulevard and accompanying water mains through the Belle Meade Company that he controlled. His father-in-law, Percy Warner, president of the Nashville Street Railway and Light Company, had earlier agreed to extend his electric streetcar line to the present-day Percy Warner Park. The street, originally macadamized, was named for the Belle Meade plantation, through which it traveled. I remember hearing of the death of President Franklin Roosevelt on April 12, 1945, while I was walking down the median strip of Belle Meade Boulevard looking for metal spikes from the electric railroad that had ceased operation on February 1, 1941.

**BELLEVUE DRIVES EAST** and **NORTH,** near Belle Meade Mansion, were part of Johnson Bransford's subdivision, the plans of which were recorded in 1923 and 1924, respectively. Bellevue means "beautiful view" and complemented Belle Meade, which means "beautiful meadow."

**BELLEVUE ROAD,** in Bellevue, runs from Old Hickory Boulevard west to Old Harding Pike. The road and the community were named for Belle Vue, the home built by Lewis DeMoss in 1797, overlooking the Harpeth River.

*Ward–Belmont College was advertised on the back of this postcard, postmarked 1924, as "perhaps the largest college for women in the South," with an enrollment of between six hundred and seven hundred. Today, Belmont University occupies the campus and has renamed the building at 1900 Belmont Boulevard, shown in the center of this picture, Freeman Hall.*

**BELMONT BOULEVARD** begins at Portland Avenue and runs south to Shackleford Road at the southern end of the David Lipscomb University campus. The street was named for Adelicia Hayes Franklin Acklen Cheatham's home, Belle Monte, that still stands on the Belmont University campus. Property along Belmont was initially developed by the Belmont Land Company, owned by James C. Bradford and A. H. Robinson. They bought the land from Mrs. Cheatham after she moved to Washington, D.C., in 1885. During the first decade of the twentieth century, the Belmont Land Company built macadamized streets and granitoid sidewalks, extended the streetcar line out Belmont Boulevard, and installed city water in what was called Belmont Heights. Belmont University president, Dr. Bob Fisher, and his wife, Judy, live on what was "lot no. 1" in Belmont Heights subdivision.

**BEN ALLEN ROAD** runs east from Dickerson Pike and south to Hart Lane. The street was named for Benjamin B. Allen (1855–1910), a local financier.

**BENTON AVENUE** is a fascinating street that empties into Eighth Avenue South two blocks south of Wedgewood. At its southern end, Benton becomes Lindell Avenue. Before Interstate 65 was built, Benton Avenue continued east to the state fairgrounds. The street was the centerpiece of the Waverly Place development of the late 1880s by the Waverly Land Company. Benton Avenue is thought to have been named for Thomas Hart Benton, and is located on what once was the farm of Tennessee historian A. W. Putnam. He lived there from the late 1830s until he sold Waverly Place in 1858 for $45,000 and moved closer to town. He named his farm for *Waverly*, the novel Sir Walter Scott completed in 1814. After Tennessee Governor Albert Roberts left office in 1921, he and his wife lived at 724 Benton Avenue before moving to a farm near Nashville. Today, the quiet street has a number of attractive homes of various architectural styles ranging from Georgian to bungalow.

**BENTON SMITH ROAD**, which curves south from Harding Place a short distance west of Granny White Pike, was named for Col. Benton Smith, CSA, of the Twentieth Tennessee Infantry. He was permanently disabled after being severely wounded in the head by a Union officer who struck him with a saber after Smith surrendered at nearby Shy's Hill during the Battle of Nashville in December 1864.

**BERNARD AVENUE**, originally known as St. Bernard Avenue, was named for its next-door neighbor to the east, St. Bernard Convent, dedicated on July 1, 1905. The street was listed in the city directory the next year, although it was outside the city limits. At that time, the city limits were at Blakemore on the west side of Hillsboro and between Acklen and Portland on the east side of the street. The first house on Bernard Avenue was occupied in 1910.

**BERRIEN STREET**, in South Nashville, was named for J. Berrien Lindsley, chancellor of the University of Nashville and founder of Montgomery Bell Academy.

**BERRY STREET** runs by McFerrin Park in East Nashville. The street was named for John Berry McFerrin (1807–87), Methodist preacher, editor, and historian.

**BLACKBURN AVENUE**, that runs from Windsor to Westover Drive in Belle Meade, and nearby Blackburn Place were both named for Luke Blackburn, the top three-year-old thoroughbred of 1880. This son of Bonnie Scotland stood (was available, for a fee, to be bred with mares) at the Belle Meade Stud from 1883 until 1904. Both streets were part of Johnson Bransford's Belle Meade Golf Links subdivision that began in 1915.

**BLACKMAN ROAD** runs from Trousdale Drive to Edmonson Pike. It was named for the Blackman family, who lived in the area.

**BLAIR BOULEVARD** runs from Sharondale east to Hillsboro Pike. It was likely named for G. W. Blair, who, with O. H. Shields, developed eighty-seven acres on Hillsboro into five-acre lots. Originally called Long Avenue, Blair Boulevard's first residents appeared in 1910. A street numbering system began three years later. Brown's Diner has been at 2102 Blair Boulevard since 1935. From 1927 until 1935, it was on the southeast corner of Blair and Hillsboro, where the Kinnard building is today.

**BLUE BRICK DRIVE**, near the Hermitage, was named for Blue Brick, a home built before 1800 about one-half mile behind the Clover Bottom plantation on what is now the corner of present-day Stewarts Ferry and Blue Brick Drive. The house received its name because one wall was painted blue.

**BLUE HOLE ROAD** crosses Mill Creek just south of its beginning at Moss Road. Past the creek, the road runs due south to terminate at Old Hickory Boulevard. Blue Hole Road was named for a large hole in Mill Creek so deep it looked blue to the youngsters who swam there. The "blue hole" is two-tenths of a mile west of the intersection of Bell Road and Interstate 24.

**BOENSCH STREET** was named by developer Dudley Warner II in the late 1990s for Dottie Frist Boensch, sister of Senator William H. Frist, MD, and Thomas F. Frist Jr., MD. It is located off of Graybar Lane just east of Hillsboro Pike.

**BONAIRE STREET** was a dirt road that led from Harding Place to the driveway of the two-story residence of Nashville Golf and Country Club golf pro George Livingston. It was built in 1915. A native of Scotland, Livingston named the street Bonaire. During the Depression, Bonaire Street was paved and extended to Forsythe Place by the Works Progress Administration. Livingston then renamed the street Highland Avenue. Later, the street was extended to Tyne Boulevard and was renamed. *See Westview Avenue.*

**BONAVENTURE PLACE** was named for Bonaventure, the home of Mr. and Mrs. Charles C. Trabue Jr., built in 1911, on the high ground next to Harding Pike in Belle Meade. Mr. Trabue was a prominent Nashville attorney.

**BONDURANT STREET**, near the Old Hickory Marina, was named for Maj. Jacob Bondurant, a French Huguenot and a major in Gen. Andrew Jackson's army. The Bondurant mansion was converted into the first clubhouse of the Old Hickory Country Club. The Bondurant family cemetery is also located on the country club property.

**"BONNA" STREETS** (Bonnabrook, Bonnacliff, Bonnacreek, and Bonnacrest) are located in the Stanford Country Club subdivision. The prefix "bonna" means beautiful. Eva Richardson named the streets.

**BONTEMPS DRIVE** is a short street between Buena Vista Pike and Whites Creek Pike. The street was named for Arnaud "Arna" Bontemps, an African

American poet, fiction writer, and member of the Harlem Renaissance. He became head librarian at Fisk University in 1943, and continued to be a productive writer during his twenty-two years at Fisk. His works include biographies of George Washington Carver, Frederick Douglas, and Booker T. Washington.

**BORDEAUX PLACE** is a short street north of West Trinity Lane and south of Moormans Arm Road. It was named for the Bordeaux community, which was named about 1889, when Dr. M. O. Randall returned from practicing dentistry in France. Perhaps Nashville's area north of the Cumberland reminded him of the French city on the Garonne River, famous for its wines.

**BOSCOBEL STREET**, formerly called Watson Street, begins at Sixth Street and continues east to Tenth Street in East Nashville. It was named for Boscobel, a house built by Dr. John Shelby for his daughter Anna. Boscobel means "beautiful grove." In 1875, the infamous outlaw Jesse James lived in a cottage on Boscobel Street under the alias J. D. Howard.

**BOSLEY SPRINGS ROAD** was named for Charles Bosley, whose vast plantation on both sides of Richland Turnpike extended from present-day White Bridge Road to the Samuel Watkins tract about eight hundred yards west of today's Hillsboro Pike. During the Civil War, Bosley made a lot of money quartering horses for the Union Army. The Bosley plantation occupied much of the Richland, Sugartree, and Kingfisher Creek watersheds as well as land where the Belle Meade Shopping Center, Saint Thomas Hospital, Aquinas College, and Montgomery Bell Academy now stand. Bosley Sulphur Spring, south of Bosley's house, was destroyed by the excavation work for Saint Thomas Hospital on Harding Pike.

**BOWLING AVENUE** begins at Murphy Road, crosses West End Avenue, and runs south to end at Woodmont Boulevard. The street was named for the Bowling family. When Gertrude Bowling Whitworth's husband, John Leonard Whitworth, died, she inherited a large tract of land that she sold for $100,000 in 1910. *See Golf Club Lane.*

**BOWLINGATE LANE** was developed in the mid-1980s by Dudley Warner II after he purchased land on Bowling Avenue from Dr. Thomas F. Frist Sr. The thirteen cluster homes are near the intersection of Bowling Avenue and Golf Club Lane. The open, divided entrance with high, cut-stone piers and gas lights have a gated appearance, but without a gate or gatehouse.

**BOYD STREET** ran from Patterson Street to West End Avenue. The street was named for John Boyd, whose home was on the property before the street was subdivided in 1858. The city limits ended at Boyd and Church Streets in 1900. Its name was changed in December 1904. *See Twentieth Avenue.*

**BRADFORD AVENUE** begins at Tenth Avenue South and runs east, crossing Franklin Pike in Melrose, before ending at Lindell Avenue. The street was named for attorney James C. Bradford, whose home, Woodstock, was close by on Franklin Pike. Mr. Bradford was an uncle of James C. Bradford, his namesake, who lived with the Bradfords in 1908, while a student at Montgomery Bell Academy (MBA). Later, the younger James C. Bradford founded J. C. Bradford and Co., a successful investment banking firm.

**BRANCH STREET** runs north from Porter Road to McGavock Pike. The road is best known for an African American community called Rock City that has long existed on the side of a hill beside the street. In the 1960s and earlier, men and women of the Rock City community worked for some of Nashville's most prominent families, gaining their respect and confidence. Horace Greeley Hill Jr. gave money each year to the Rock City Men's Club and, by doing so, helped Rock City finally acquire city utilities. Mrs. Lucius Burch, who employed Edward Boleyjack at her home, Riverwood, was also helpful to the Rock City community.

**BRANDAU PLACE** begins at Twenty-Third Avenue North and runs two blocks south to Twenty-Fifth Avenue North. The street was named for Roberta and Adolph Gustav Brandau, who moved into a house at 201 Twenty-Third Avenue North, at the corner of Brandau Place, in 1901. Mr. Brandau owned Brandau Printing Company.

**BRANSFORD AVENUE** runs from Wedgewood Avenue to Berry Road west of the state fairgrounds. The street was named for Louise Bransford, daughter of William Bransford, who lived at Melrose on Franklin Pike.

**BRENNER DRIVE**, off Morton Mill Road in Bellevue, was named for a grandchild of the developer of the subdivision.

**BREWER DRIVE** runs southeast from Edmonson Pike to Nolensville Pike. Local developers Robert T. Coleman and his father, Samuel F. Coleman, named the street for Jim Brewer, who was also in the real estate business.

**BRICK CHURCH PIKE** begins at Trinity Lane, immediately west of the Interstates 24 and 65 interchange. The road runs north and then east to its intersection with Dickerson Road. The Brick Church Turnpike Company began constructing the pike in 1850. It was named for a two-story brick church that once stood six miles north of the intersection of Brick Church Lane and Brick Church Pike.

**BRIGHTWOOD AVENUE** begins at Rosewood Avenue and runs south to Stokes Lane. Near its southern end, it crosses over Interstate 440. The street carries the name of Brightwood, the home Joseph Hamilton Thompson built in 1877 on today's Thompson Lane near 100 Oaks Mall.

**BRILEY PARKWAY** was named for Beverly Briley, the first mayor of the Metropolitan Government of Nashville and Davidson County (1963–75). Briley proposed the road as a unifying route around the perimeter of Davidson County. The first leg of the parkway, between Elm Hill Pike and Vultee Boulevard, opened in 1961. The last section, a 1.6 mile stretch between Interstates 24 and 65 north of the city, opened thirty-six years later on December 19, 1997.

**BROADWAY**, originally named Broad Street, was laid out in 1803 when Cumberland College land was divided into lots and sold. This street, named because of its width, was then given by the college to the city. When Nashville was snow-covered, such as on January 30, 1895, Broad Street from the Custom House to the river was a favorite sledding spot. In the early 1900s, there was a large watering trough at the foot of Broad Street for horses. In 1906, Broad Street became the dividing line between north and south avenues on the west side of the river. (Church Street had been the previous dividing line.) On October 2, 1907, a mammoth parade featuring "Buffalo Bill" Cody and his Wild West Show came down Broad Street to Centennial Park. In 1911, the speed limit on Broad was fifteen miles per hour. Since the 1930s, city maps show Broad

*This 1900 street–level view of Broadway shows Union Station under construction. The wooden bridge would soon be replaced by a modern steel viaduct built by the Terminal Company. In the background are the Nashville, Chattanooga & St. Louis Railroad office building, built in 1881, on the left, and the Vaulxhall Annex, built in 1882, on the right.*
KERMIT C. STENGEL JR. COLLECTION

Street's official name to be Broadway. Some people think that Broadway ends at Sixteenth Avenue and becomes West End at that point. Sixteenth is where West End starts, but Broadway continues to Twenty-First Avenue South at the eastern edge of the Vanderbilt University campus.

**BROOK HOLLOW ROAD** begins at Charlotte Pike and runs south to dead-end at US Highway 70 South. Along its hilly course, the road crosses Ewin Branch and Jocelyn Hollow Branch, two small creeks that may have suggested the name.

**BROWNLEE DRIVE**, in West Meade, was named for Brownlee O. Currey, one of the developers of West Meade in 1944. Mr. Currey was a founder and

*This early twentieth-century postcard view of Broadway hints at the affluence of this residential street. The tower of Moore Memorial Presbyterian Church at 1507-09 Broadway is on the right. The church was dedicated on March 22, 1874. In 1936, the congregation voted to buy a new church site at 3900 West End Avenue and change the church name to Westminster Presbyterian. Union Station is the building in the distance.*

RIDLEY WILLS II COLLECTION

longtime chairman of the board of Equitable Securities, a Nashville-based investment banking company that, for two decades, was the dominant bond house in the South.

BRUSH HILL ROAD occupies high ground along the bluff of the Cumberland River in Inglewood. Its northern end is a dead end between the river and Cheek Lake. Its other end is just north of McGavock Pike. Some of the attractive homes on Brush Hill Road were part of the Riverwood subdivision built in the 1930s. Business executives, such as Owen Howell Jr., president of Genesco, had homes on Brush Hill Road where, in their back yards, they could enjoy the cool air off of the river. Mr. and Mrs. Thomas W. Schlater Jr. also lived on the street with their two children, Tommy and Mary.

Mr. Schlater was a respected attorney. In the 1930s, the Schlaters erected a fence across the back of their property to keep their children from falling into the Cumberland River. Mrs. Schlater didn't learn until years later that Tommy had found a hole in the fence.

**BUENA VISTA PIKE** begins at Tucker Road close to West Trinity Lane. It runs north to its intersection with Whites Creek Pike (US Highway 431). The Buena Vista Turnpike Company was incorporated in 1849 to build a road that commenced near the north end of Spruce Street and continued northwest to cross the Cumberland on the Buena Vista Ferry (earlier called Barrow's Ferry). From there, the pike went through agricultural lands in Whites Creek Valley to a point about five miles from Nashville. The turnpike was named after the Battle of Buena Vista fought during the Mexican War near Saltillo, a city in northeastern Mexico, on February 22, 1847.

**BUCHANAN STREET** runs east from Eighth Avenue North to Ed Temple Boulevard in North Nashville. It was probably named for early settlers, Alex and John Buchanan, who came to the Cumberland settlements from South Carolina in about 1780.

**BURCHWOOD AVENUE** runs west from Gallatin Pike to Gear Street. It was the result of the subdivision of the Burch estate on Gallatin Pike in August 1929.

**BURKITT ROAD** begins at Nolensville Pike near the Davidson-Williamson County line. The road runs east to Cane Ridge, where it swerves to the north before becoming part of Old Hickory Boulevard. The road was named for Dr. Andrew Jackson Burkitt's family. He graduated from the medical department of the University of Nashville in 1879.

**BURLINGTON** is the name for both a "court" and a "place" just off of Hobbs Road. They were named for Burlington, the beautiful home of the Elliston family, the plans for which were developed by William Strickland. Joseph T. Elliston died before the home was completed by his son, William R. Elliston, in 1850. The house faced the Richland Turnpike with a double line of cedar trees bordering the walk from the front door to the road. During the Civil War, all the fences and all but two of the trees at Burlington were used by the Federals for firewood.

**BURTON AVENUE** is a short street on the west side of Belmont Boulevard that runs east to quickly dead-end into Observatory Drive. The street was named for A. M. Burton, the founder of Life and Casualty Insurance Company of Tennessee and a major benefactor of David Lipscomb College (now a university), whose campus is on the east side of Belmont Boulevard.

**BURTON HILLS BOULEVARD**, in Green Hills, is in the shape of a half circle with both ends facing west at Hillsboro Pike. The boulevard was named for the Andrew Mizell Burton family who lived there in the old Felix Compton house from 1929 until 1958, when the house and thirty-five acres passed into the ownership of David Lipscomb College. During the beginning of the Battle of Nashville on December 15, 1864, the Compton house was used by the Confederates as a field hospital. The next day, in the hills southeast of the house, the Confederate Army of Tennessee was decisively defeated, ending the battle. In the summer of 1984, over 170 years after the oldest part of the house had been built, a corporation headed by Jerry Carroll bought the tract and adjoining land, removed the residence, and soon developed a mixed residential/commercial development called Burton Hills.

**CALDWELL LANE** runs between Granny White and Franklin Pikes in the Glendale section of Nashville. It was named for the James E. Caldwell family who lived at Longview on Franklin Pike at Caldwell Lane. Glendale Park was established on sixty-four acres at the intersection of present-day Caldwell Lane and Lealand Lane in 1887 as Woodstock Park. Renamed Glendale Park in 1890, it was the creation of James E. Caldwell and Oscar Noel Sr., who headed the Waverly Land Development Company which constructed the "dummy" streetcar line to the park. (A small steam locomotive pulled the train's cars.)

In about 1900, Noel donated twenty-five acres south of Caldwell Lane on the dummy line to Elizabeth Burgess Buford so that she could build a college for young ladies on the property. He also agreed to construct buildings on the campus. The only condition was that, after Mrs. Buford's death, the site was to return to Noel's heirs. Buford College opened in 1901 as a school for "cultured, Christian women to the manor born."[7] By 1911, the school had one hundred students and a second building, Burgess Hall, which opened in about 1908. When Noel died, Mrs. Buford may have felt pressure from his heirs to move the school. She did so to two or three Nashville mansions between 1916 and 1920.

Mrs. Buford's health declined suddenly in January 1920, and she died soon thereafter. Her college perished with her.

**CALIFORNIA AVENUE** was named for the state in hopes of attracting people from there to the new town of West Nashville. Laid out in 1887, California Avenue runs from Centennial Boulevard to Sixty-Third Avenue North. Along with many other streets between Centennial Boulevard and Interstate 40 named for states, California Avenue is part of "The Nations," as it is referred to by area residents. This area is so called because of the 1792 treaty the settlers signed with the Cherokee, Chickasaw, and Choctaw tribes at Treaty Oak that then stood where Louisiana Avenue crosses Sixty-Second Avenue. *See Wyoming Avenue.*

**CANE RIDGE ROAD** runs southeast from Cedar Pointe Parkway to Old Hickory Boulevard in Antioch. It was named because of its location on a high ridge that was covered with cane brakes.

**CANTERBURY DRIVE** runs from West Brookfield south to its intersection with Nichol Lane near the Percy Warner Golf Course. When built, the street was advertized as part of the Highlands of Belle Meade, developed by the Belle Meade Land Company soon after the plat was recorded on August 21, 1928. When I was a little boy in the late 1930s, I was allowed to ride my tricycle on Canterbury because, having only three houses at the other end of the street, traffic was almost non-existent.

**CANTRELL AVENUE** runs north from Woodmont to Oaklawn Avenue. It was named for the developer who subdivided the northern part of the street.

**CAPERS AVENUE**, one block north of and parallel to Blakemore Avenue, was relatively unknown until resident Miss Fannie Mae Dees decided to fight the University Center Urban Renewal project that was threatening her neighborhood. Ultimately, Vanderbilt prevailed and, by 1980, only two of nearly six hundred residents remained, still fighting in the courts to keep their properties. Fannie Mae Dees, who died in 1978, is remembered by the Fannie Mae Dees Park established later that year in her honor. The 7.6-acre park fronts on Blakemore Avenue and Twenty-Fourth Avenue South. *See Children's Way.*

**CAPITOL BOULEVARD** was built in 1910 to connect Church Street with the State Capitol. The city council had, in 1909, passed an ordinance condemning thirty-five feet on either side of the existing ten-foot wide Capitol Alley to make the street possible. The battle cry of advocates of the eighty-foot-wide boulevard was, "Rescue the Capitol from a back street."[8] This worked and the Tennessee General Assembly approved the project for which the city would bear most of the cost. With the completion of the boulevard in 1910, passengers in automobiles driving from Church to Cedar Street (now Charlotte Avenue) had an unobstructed view of the State Capitol, considered one of the most perfect public buildings in the country.

*This victory parade down Capitol Boulevard took place soon after the end of World War I. The name of silent movie star George Walsh is displayed on the marquee of the Knickerbocker Theater on the right. Also shown are the Castner-Knott department store on the left, and the Orpheum Theater at 210 Seventh Avenue North, the YMCA, the State Capitol, and the Hermitage Hotel.*
KERMIT C. STENGEL JR. COLLECTION

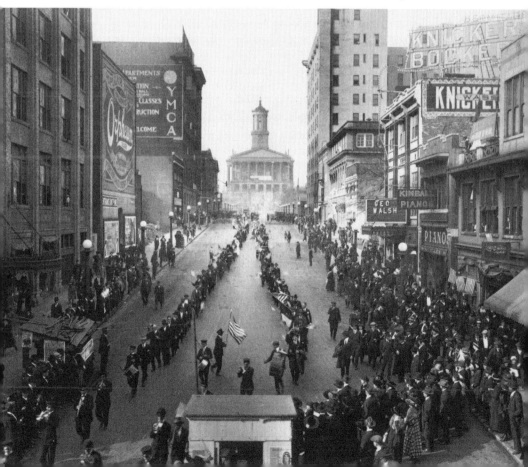

**CARDEN AVENUE** runs from West End Avenue to Rolland Road. The street was subdivided by the Bransford Realty Company, who recorded the plat on July 23, 1924. Carden Avenue was named for Martha Ann Carden, daughter of Allen D. Carden and wife of Charles Bosley Jr.

**CARGILE** is the name for both a "lane" and a "road" in West Meade. They were named for Neil Cargile, who lived in a house his father-in-law, William F. Allen, built following the purchase of the 1,750-acre West Meade Farm in 1944 by a group of Nashville businessmen, including Cargile, E. A. Wortham, Brownlee O. Currey, and Ronald L. Voss. *See Sedberry Road.*

**CARL MILLER DRIVE,** between Nolensville Pike and Old Hickory Boulevard, north of Barnes Road, was named for Carl Miller, who was employed by the Metro Codes Administration.

**CARROLL STREET** ran, in 1898, from Market Street five blocks east to Wharf Avenue. Peabody Normal School campus was one block north. The street was probably named for William Carroll, governor of Tennessee from 1821 to 1827 and from 1829 to 1835. He is buried in nearby City Cemetery. Today, Carroll Street is broken up with portions on both sides of Lafayette Street. Carroll Street was earlier named Asylum Street.

**CASCADE DRIVE** begins at Saundersville Road and runs south to Lebanon Pike, east of Andrew Jackson Parkway. Cascade Drive has the same name as the mountain range that runs through Oregon and Washington.

**CASTLEMAN DRIVE** parallels Hobbs Road, one block to the south. It begins at Lindawood Drive and runs east to Belmont Park Terrace. The drive was named for Andrew Castleman, who lived several hundred yards to the north.

**CATO ROAD** runs northwest from Hydes Ferry Pike in the Jordonia area. It crosses Briley Parkway and ends several miles to the northwest. The road was named for Rolin Cato or another member of the Cato family who resided on the road.

**CATSKILL DRIVE** is located on the eastern edge of Davidson County and extends into Wilson County. It shares the name with the Catskill Mountains of New York.

CEDAR LANE was named by attorney Walter Stokes when he constructed it through the northern portion of his property in about 1907. It was named for the cedar trees that covered Montgomery Hill, where Col. A. B. Montgomery's mansion once stood east of Hillsboro Pike. The entrance to the house was on Granny White Pike, from which a long carriageway, lined with cedar trees, led to the house that was on the corner of today's Cedar Lane and Brightwood Avenue. Montgomery burned the house in December 1864 to prevent it from being seized by Federal troops. A narrow, two-story brick house survives from the Montgomery era at 1806 Cedar Lane.

CEDAR STREET was one of the streets in the 1784 Molloy plan that ran east and west. It began at the public square and ran west by the cedar knob for which it was named. During the decade of the 1840s, the post office was at Cedar and Cherry. As there was no delivery then, citizens went to the post office to pick up their mail that came by boat or stage. In 1854, Cedar Street became Charlotte Turnpike at McLemore Street.

*This 1880s photograph of Cedar Street looks down the hill and east, toward St. Mary's Catholic Church at the corner of Summer and Cedar Streets. In 1868, the church purchased the house in the foreground, which was built by George Washington Campbell.*

RIDLEY WILLS II COLLECTION

"Hell's Half Acre" was a low-lying area on Cedar Street (today's Charlotte Pike) at the bottom of the hill along the railroad tracks north of the Nashville, Chattanooga & St. Louis (N. C. & St. L.) depot. The area was inhabited by African Americans who, because of deplorable living conditions, were susceptible to contagious diseases. Understandably, crime was prevalent. *See Charlotte Pike.*

**CEMENT PLANT ROAD** runs beside the Cumberland River in North Nashville just upstream from the Interstate 65 bridge. It was named for the Hermitage-Portland Cement Plant to which the road led. In the flood of December 1926–January 1927, that reached 56.4 feet at the foot of Broadway, the cement plant was completely surrounded by water and shut down. The site was occupied in 2011 by Metro Water Services.

**CENTENNIAL BOULEVARD** was surveyed by W. H. Lyle about the time of the Tennessee Centennial Celebration in 1897. The road ran from the end of Jefferson Street to the state penitentiary. The street was also called Esplanade Boulevard because it ran near the bluff of the Cumberland River. The "Esplanade" name was soon dropped because it seemed a little too elegant for a neighborhood that included inexpensive housing for prison workers and families of inmates. The name "Centennial" may have been chosen by the state officials who financed the project. It is thought, however, that Capt. Mark Sterling Cockrill, who was president of the Nashville Land Improvement Company in 1896, suggested the name. By 1900, chemical, fertilizer, lumber, phosphate, and storage companies lined the riverbank across the railroad tracks beside Centennial Boulevard.

**CHALMERS DRIVE** runs south from Harding Place equidistant from Hillsboro and Granny White Pikes. Near Shy's Hill, the street was named for Gen. James R. Chalmers, CSA, who fought in the Battle of Nashville on December 15–16, 1864.

**CHAMBERLIN STREET** runs south from Elkins Avenue to Sentinel Drive. The street, formerly part of Thirty-Eighth Avenue North, was renamed for James N. Chamberlin, a railroad mail clerk, who owned rental houses on the street and was a benevolent landlord. Mayor Hilliary House learned about Mr. Chamberlin's goodwill, and renamed the section of Thirty-Eighth Avenue North for him, possibly in the late 1920s.

**CHANNELKIRK LANE** is located off of Graybar Lane just east of Hillsboro Pike. It was named by developer Dudley Warner II in the late 1990s for Channelkirk Cottage, a three-hundred-year-old house in Scotland, owned at the time by friends of the Warners. *See Oxton Hill Lane.*

**CHARLES DRIVE** is just north of Old Hickory Boulevard and midway between Interstate 65 North and Gallatin Pike. In 1972, its name was changed from Chelsea Drive to Charles Drive in memory of Charles Headley, who was killed in Vietnam in February 1968.

**CHARLES E. DAVIS BOULEVARD** runs north from Lafayette Street to Carroll Street. It was named for the former Vanderbilt and NBA star, youth advocate, and founder of the Charles Davis Foundation who grew up in this neighborhood.

**CHARLOTTE PIKE** (US Highway 70) was named for Charlotte Reeves Robertson, wife of Gen. James Robertson, cofounder of Nashville. The road was constructed in 1804 by Robertson and his slaves. In town, Charlotte Pike was originally known as Cedar Street. Charlotte was the main road leading west from Nashville to Charlotte, Tennessee (also named for Mrs. Robertson). The Charlotte Turnpike was chartered in 1831. Before the Civil War, James Dungey, a free black, ran the tollhouse on the pike. He and his family lived in a log cabin at 3307 Charlotte Pike. Further out, at the corner of what is now Fifty-First Avenue and Charlotte Pike, Byrd Douglas built a mansion on his plantation in 1848. He and his brother, Hugh, made their fortunes from their cotton warehouse downtown. In 1898, there was a coliseum and bicycle track on the north side of Charlotte Turnpike between Charlotte and Old Charlotte Road.

A short distance beyond today's Centennial Medical Complex, Charlotte climbs Dungey's Hill. Further west, in the heart of West Nashville, Richland Park faces Charlotte from the south side between Forty-Sixth and Fiftieth Avenues North. The park was laid out as a village green by the Nashville Land Improvement Company in 1887, and presented to the citizens of West Nashville that same year. West Nashville was annexed into the City of Nashville in 1906.

Early in the twentieth century, the east side of Dungey's Hill was the center of railroad activity with the N. C. & St. L. Railroad's new shops to the south of Charlotte and the Tennessee Central's Van Blocken Station on the side of the hill. Tony Sudekum's Crescent Amusement Company opened the Elite Theater on Charlotte across from Richland Park in 1927. There were two shows a day and a Seeburg organ played during intermission. *See Cedar Street.*

CHEEK ROAD extends from Highway 100 to Page Road. It was named for the Leslie Cheek family, who built Cheekwood in 1929. In 1969, the Cheeks' daughter, Hulda Cheek Sharp, and her husband, Walter Sharp, gave the estate to the state of Tennessee. Cheekwood, which has an entrance on Cheek Road, is now the Cheekwood Botanical Gardens and Fine Arts Center.

CHEROKEE AVENUE, south of Trinity Lane in East Nashville, was named for a Native American tribe who lived in Tennessee. The Cherokees had villages in North and South Carolina, Alabama, Georgia, and Tennessee. The Cherokee Park neighborhood, located between West End Avenue, Cherokee Road, the CSX railroad tracks, and North Wilson Boulevard, was developed by the Wakefield-Davis Realty Company in 1928. The famous Olmstead Brothers, landscape architects, designed the curving streets that included Lauderdale, Mayfair, and Mockingbird Roads. In 2000, the Metro Council approved a controversial protective zoning overlay for the neighborhood designed to protect approximately three hundred homes, many of which are Tudor Revival–style structures built from the late 1920s to the 1950s. In 2004, attractive street signs were installed. They included the words "Historic Cherokee Park est. 1928" and a profile of a typical Cherokee Park home.

CHERRY STREET (now Fourth Avenue) between College Street (now Third Avenue) and Summer Street (now Fifth Avenue), was named for Cherry Street in Philadelphia. Some of the Scots-Irish who settled in Nashville came down the Shenandoah Valley from Pennsylvania. Additionally, many early Nashville merchants bought their supplies in Philadelphia.

The first street railroad company, incorporated on March 19, 1860, constructed its lines soon after the close of the Civil War. The mule-drawn streetcar went south on Cherry Street to Chestnut Street and back on College Street to Cedar Street. At the end of the war, Cherry and other principal Nashville streets were in a delapidated condition due to the constant and heavy hauling done by immense numbers of Union army wagons and the passing to and fro of heavy artillery, ambulances, and other army vehicles. Cherry Street south of City Cemetery was impassible. In the spring of 1866, the southern portion of the street was macadamized, and the portion between Church and Cedar Streets was paved with an experimental "Nicholson pavement." At about the same time, wooden sidewalks were put down on Cherry in the downtown area.

In the 1880s, the Maxwell House Hotel, at the corner of Cherry (now Fourth Avenue North) and Church Streets, was considered to be the heart of Nashville. At that street crossing, the busiest in the town, there was a turntable in the middle of Cherry Street, where the little mules turned their cars around to go in different directions. The mule cart drivers knew the town and where everybody lived, and were supplements to the very crude city directory.

In the 1890s, Cherry Street, between Church and Union, was known as the "Men's Quarter." It featured several gambling houses, including the Southern Turf and the Climax Saloon, and a six-story, Italianate hotel called the Utopia, built in the 1890s in anticipation of the crowds that would be attracted by the 1897 Tennessee Centennial Celebration. Cherry Street's name was changed by the city council in December 1904.

Black Bottom was a low-lying area between Rutledge Hill and Broad Street and between the river and south Cherry Street (now Fourth Avenue South). The flood-prone section was inhabited by African Americans. A notorious business in Black Bottom was a "barrel house" that sold whiskey from barrels on racks along the walls. The bartender would pour the whiskey out of wooden spigots into bottles for the customers. One saloon was called the Bucket of Blood. About 1900, a part of Black Bottom was converted into the Hay Market, where farmers came on Saturdays to sell hay and trade horses. *See Fourth Avenue.*

CHET ATKINS PLACE was named in honor of the country music producer, guitarist, and singer when South Street between Sixteenth and Twentieth Avenues South was renamed in 1991.

CHICKASAW AVENUE, south of Trinity Lane in East Nashville, was named for a Native American tribe. The Chickasaws primarily lived in North Mississippi and hunted in West Tennessee. Memphis is located on the Fourth Chickasaw Bluff near the mouth of the Wolf River.

CHICKERING ROAD runs from Belle Meade Boulevard past Percy Warner Park to Old Hickory Boulevard. The road and Chickering Lane, an extension

*This view, looking north on Cherry Street (Fourth Avenue North) from Church Street, shows the Maxwell House Hotel on the left.*

*ARTWORK OF NASHVILLE, 1894–1901*

of Chickering Road, were named for the Chickering family who lived in the neighborhood in the 1820s. Judge John Chickering, of Richland Creek, was a friend of William Giles Harding, of Belle Meade.

CHILDREN'S WAY runs northwest from Twenty-First Avenue South to Natchez Trace. The street's name was changed from Capers Avenue after Vanderbilt University completed the Monroe Carell Jr. Children's Hospital on the street in February 2004. *See Capers Avenue.*

CHOCTAW TRACE, off of Neelys Bend Road, was named for a Native American tribe in North Mississippi. In 1830, the Choctaws traded their land to the United States for new land in Oklahoma. Settlers quickly bought the land west of the Tombigbee River near Columbus, Mississippi.

CHURCH STREET was named for the churches built through the years on what was originally named Spring Street. They included a Methodist Church on the north side between Cherry Street and Black Horse or Printer's Alley; the Presbyterian Church at Summer Street; Christ Church at the northeast corner of High Street; and a Baptist church, which later became a Christian church, where the Nashville Public Library is today. People began to unofficially call the area "Church Street." The name change became official on June 28, 1866. Church Street later was extended west to the city limits at Boyd Avenue (now Twentieth Avenue North). At that point, the road became Richland Turnpike, later Harding Turnpike.

Granite paving, the first in Nashville, was laid on Church Street, from Cherry to Vine, at the end of 1887. When West Side Park, which featured two racetracks, a grandstand and club house, opened that same year, its main entrance was near the end of Church Street at present-day Brandau Place and Twenty-Fifth Avenue North. The park became the home of the Tennessee Centennial Celebration in 1897 and is today's Centennial Park.

The demolition of the Demoville home in 1902, at the corner of Church and Vine Streets, marked the end of Church Street east of the railroad gulch as a residential area. Work on changing the gauge of the streetcar tracks on Church Street from broad to standard gauge began in 1903. In 1911, the speed limit on Church Street was fifteen miles per hour.

For many years in the middle of the twentieth century, Candyland, on the southeast corner of Church Street and Seventh Avenue, was a favorite spot for

*This 1941 view looks west on Church Street, showing Cain-Sloan Company on the northwest corner of Fifth Avenue North. Because electric streetcars downtown had only recently been replaced by gasoline-powered city buses, the streetcar rails had not yet been removed. The crowds on the north side of the street are waiting for a parade.*

KERMIT C. STENGEL JR. COLLECTION

Hume Fogg students and teenagers from other schools. Candyland served sand-wiches, limeades, chocolate drifts, and other luscious ice cream delights. *See Spring Street.*

CLARENDON AVENUE begins at Harding Pike. The road fords Richland Creek and runs southeast to Belle Meade Boulevard. The street was named for Clarendon, a bay horse by imported St. Blaise out of Clara. The horse was purchased by Gen. W. H. Jackson in 1892, and stood at the Belle Meade Stud from the 1893 through the 1900 seasons.

CLARKSVILLE PIKE begins at Buchanan Street in North Nashville. It crosses the Cumberland River on the Bordeaux Bridge, built in 1917 (succeeding an earlier one built in 1889). A few miles further northwest, the highway crosses Old Hickory Boulevard before climbing Germantown Ridge and continuing on through Pleasant View to Clarksville, a distance of forty-two miles. The 1934 Highway Map of Tennessee, published by the Department of Highways and Public Works, identified the road as both US 41 and State Highway 112. An alternative route to Clarksville was through Ashland City on State Highway 12. It was seven miles longer than the US 41 route.

CLAY STREET, in North Nashville, runs from Metrocenter Boulevard to Dominican Drive. It was named for Henry Clay of Kentucky, who was a candi-date for president of the United States in 1824, 1832, and 1844.

CLEESES FERRY ROAD originally ran south from Scottsboro to Cleese's Ferry on the Cumberland River in Bell's Bend, and from there to the Charlotte Turnpike just opposite the Cockrill homeplace. The road has only two small segments left, having largely been replaced by Old Hickory Boulevard. The ferry and the road were named for the seven Cleese brothers who came to this section in the 1860s, and who owned land in Whites Bend (later Bell's Bend). J. N. Cleese and two partners laid out the road from the river south to the Charlotte Turnpike in about 1871. When the Williamson Ferry upstream became obsolete in 1965, the ferry boat there, the *Judge Litton Hickman*, moved downstream to replace the smaller craft at Cleese's Ferry. To accommodate the *Judge Litton Hickman*, the river had to be dredged at that point to make it navi-gable. Cleese's Ferry ceased operation in 1987.

**CLENDENIN ROAD** is a north-south road between Stonewall Drive and Gateway Lane. The street is on what once was part of the Lealand estate. Clendenin Road was named for William Clendenin Robertson, a Texan who was the 1893 valedictorian at the University of the South in Sewanee. That fall, he tutored Overton and Luke Lea. The friendship that developed between Robertson and the Leas would last for their lifetimes. Clendenin married Luke and Overton's sister, Laura Lea, and later became an Episcopal priest.

**CLEVELAND STREET** runs east from Dickerson Pike to McFerrin Avenue. The street was presumably named for President Grover Cleveland.

**CLIFTON AVENUE** is the home of Swett's Restaurant. The street runs from Spruce Street, only yards off of Charlotte Pike, to Fortieth Avenue North. Originally, the road connected the village of Clifton (laid out in 1858) and its landing on the Cumberland River with the Charlotte Turnpike. Clifton became "New Town," and later part of West Nashville that was annexed by Nashville in 1906.

**CLINTON STREET** runs north from Watkins Park at Sixteenth Avenue, by the Marathon Motor Works, to Eleventh Avenue North. In 1858 and 1859, Hardin P. Bostick had two land sales of his property that ran north from the Charlotte Turnpike to the Nashville and Northwestern Railroad track. Some of those lots were on Clinton Street.

**COCHRAN DRIVE** near Hogan Road was named for Carmack Cochran, a prominent Nashville attorney who was chairman of the ten-member charter commission that recommended metropolitan government in 1958.

**COCKRILL STREET** runs northeast from Dr. D. B. Todd Boulevard to Eleventh Avenue North. The street was named for the Mark Robertson Cockrill family, prominent in early Nashville history. Cockrill's Bend of the Cumberland River is also named for this family.

**COLEY DAVIS ROAD** begins at US Highway 70 South, near Harpeth River Park. The road ends further west at the Harpeth River. It was named for Coley

Davis, a Davidson County native and Bellevue resident. He served as chairman of the Davidson County Democratic Primary Board and as a magistrate in the Nineteenth Civil District. Davis also was Davidson County jail superintendent for twenty years.

**COLICE JEANNE ROAD** runs from US Highway 70 South in Bellevue to Patten Lane. The street was named for the daughter of Mr. Corbitt, business manager for the Davidson County school system. Colice Jeanne Corbitt was said to have been born on the day the road was completed.

**COLLEGE STREET** was named because it led to Cumberland College on College Hill south of the town. The main building at the college directly faced the street's southern end. In 1866, College Street from Broad to the public square was macadamized, and put in excellent condition. When the town was blanketed with heavy snows, crowds enjoyed sledding down College Hill all the way to Broad. In 1891, plans were announced for a new streetcar transfer

*This Civil War view of Nashville from Rutledge Hill shows College Street on the right. The most visible buildings downtown are, from left to right, the State Capitol, the twin towers of the First Presbyterian Church, and the Maxwell House Hotel. The two-story building on the east side of College Street is the Medical Department of the University of Nashville.*

LIBRARY OF CONGRESS COLLECTION

station between the car shed and College Street which was renamed in December 1904.

The Hay Market was an open square established about 1900 in "Black Bottom" between College Street (now Third Avenue) and Cherry Street (now Fourth Avenue South). Its only structure was a large watering trough for animals. Farmers would arrive on Saturday mornings in their mule- or horse-driven wagons to sell or trade horses, mules, and cows. The large amounts of hay brought there to feed the animals or to sell gave the market its name. *See Third Avenue.*

**COLLINS ROAD** in Bellevue was named for Jesse Collins, a railroad engineer from Kentucky who lived in Bellevue.

**COLORADO AVENUE** runs east from McCabe Golf Course to Fortieth Avenue North. In 1927, the city of Nashville bought 131 acres of pasture and farm land from Warren Sloan to build a new airport that would be named for Lt. Brower McConnell, a Nashville native, and member of the 105th Squadron, Tennessee National Guard, who was killed on June 13, 1927, while on flying maneuvers at Langley Field, Virginia. The property was bordered on the south by the N. C. & St. L. Railroad, on the north by Colorado Avenue, on the west by Richland Creek, and on the east by greenhouses on Westlawn Avenue.

Two hangers were moved to McConnell Field and two small offices were built. One was for Louis Gasser's Nashville Flying Service and the other was for Frank J. Miller's Miller Flying Service. Nashville's first regularly scheduled airline service was inaugurated by the US Post Office Department on December 1, 1928, at McConnell Field. The Fairchild FC-2W took off with two passengers and 7,500 airmail letters. In 1930, American Airlines began to expand from Fairchild FC-2s into Curtiss Condors and, subsequently, DC-2s, which McConnell Field could not handle.

American, with some help from the state, developed a new airport called Sky Harbor twenty-five miles from Nashville between Smyrna and Murfreesboro. The 105th Squadron followed American to Sky Harbor. McConnell continued as Nashville's airport until 1937, when Berry Field opened. The City of Nashville then gave McConnell Field to the City Park System. It eventually became McCabe Golf Course.

**COMET DRIVE** between Annex Avenue and Galaxie Drive, is one of many streets in West Nashville that was named for an automobile produced by the Ford Motor Company after the automobile manufacturer established a $10 million glass plant in West Nashville in 1956. Other Ford-inspired streets in the area are Capri Drive, Continental Drive, Cougar Drive, Edsel Drive, Fordomatic Drive, Futura Drive, Galaxie Drive, Henry Ford Drive, Landau Drive, Marauder Drive, Mercomatic Drive, Premier Court, Ranchero Drive, Sprint Drive, Starliner Drive, Sunliner Drive, and Thunderbird Drive. *See River Rouge Drive.*

**COMMERCE STREET** was originally called Cumberland Alley. Named because of the commercial activity along the street, it runs from Second Avenue North to Ninth Avenue North and is lined with high-rise commercial buildings.

**COMPTON ROAD** was named for the Compton family that first came to Davidson County in 1799. In the next generation were brothers Henry and Felix Compton. They lived further out on the eastern headwaters of Richland Creek.

**CONCRETE BOULEVARD** was built as a private road by E. L. Hampton, G. A. Puryear, and realtor W. H. Armistead in 1914. It extended over Hampton's and Puryear's properties from Harding Pike to Hillsboro Pike a distance of 2.3 miles, and was advertised as the first concrete road built south of the Ohio River. Henry E. Richardson and William Jordan, the contractors, built a roadway thirty-two feet wide on a concrete slab six inches thick. The road was excavated and graded with mule-drawn wheelers. The cement, made of Cumberland River sand and gravel, was delivered in 94-pound bags and mixed at the site. The wet concrete was leveled by hand in thirty-foot sections separated by expansion joints, consisting of two steel plates separated by felt an inch thick. Because the concrete settled, cars traveling the road thumped loudly at each joint. In 1916, the name of the road was changed to Woodmont Boulevard. *See Valley Brook Road* and *Woodmont Boulevard.*

**CORNWELL AVENUE**, in Belle Meade, was part of the Berkeley Hills subdivision developed by Bransford Realty Company in the 1920s. W. B. Southgate was the surveyor. The street shares the name of Cornwall in southwest England.

**COUCHVILLE PIKE** stretches in broken segments from Donelson Pike east of the Nashville Metropolitan Airport to Rutherford County beyond Percy Priest

*This 1914 view of Concrete Boulevard (Woodmont Boulevard) shows African American laborers preparing the roadbed for the next section of concrete slab. The view looks west from near present-day Valley Brook Road and shows the fields of Gus Puryear's farm, Woodmont, to the left.*

PAUL CLEMENTS COLLECTION

Lake. The lake flooded much of this road that was named for the Couchville community in southeast Davidson County.

**COUNTY HOSPITAL ROAD** runs from John Mallette Drive in Bordeaux to Briley Parkway. The street was named for the Bordeaux Hospital on the west side of the road. In 1928, the road from Bordeaux was called Asylum Avenue. It extended only to the county poor farm and insane asylum then at the location of today's hospital.

**CONVENT PLACE** runs directly behind St. Bernard's School, from Fairfax to Bernard Avenue. Named for St. Bernard Convent, the street first appeared in the city directory in 1910.

**CRAIGHEAD AVENUE** runs north and south from Westbrook to Rolland Road. It was named for John Brown Craighead, son-in-law of Joseph Erwin, whose plantation, Peach Blossom, was on both sides of the Richland Turnpike. Erwin's daughter, Jane, married Craighead two years after her first husband, Charles Dickinson, was killed in a duel with Andrew Jackson. In 1811, Erwin gave Jane and John 194 acres across the road, where they built their two-story brick home that stands today. Jane Whitland Realty Company subdivided several lots along Craighead Avenue in 1923 and 1924.

**CRATER HILL DRIVE** climbs a hill off Lynnwood Boulevard, south of Tyne. It was named for the crater on the crest of the hill. This depression was perhaps three or four feet deep and was lined with stones. Charles Roos, who lives nearby, feels it was man-made, possibly in December 1864 to hold an artillery piece used by Union forces to shell Confederate forces on Shy's Hill to the northeast. Development has obliterated the so-called crater.

**CREIGHTON AVENUE**, between Scott Avenue and Porter Road in East Nashville, was named for Robert T. Creighton, who purchased fifteen acres located on the southwest corner of Porter Road and Creighton Street and built a large one-and-one-half-story frame house. His son, Wilbur Creighton, later wrote, "It was the first time all the children had private rooms."[9]

**CRIEVE ROAD** runs east from Regent Drive to Trousdale Drive. The road was named for Crieve Hall, a mansion built by Jesse Maxwell Overton in 1900. After living there for twenty-five years, Overton sold the home, then called Overton Hall, to Mr. and Mrs. Herbert Farrell, who renamed the home Crieve Hall. Sometime after Mr. Farrell's death in 1947, the house was torn down to make way for a subdivision.

**CROUCH DRIVE** parallels Buena Vista Pike to the east. It was named for Hubert B. Crouch, former dean at Tennessee State University.

CRUTCHER STREET runs from South Second Street in a curve paralleling the Cumberland River to deadend at South Twelfth Street. The street was named for Dr. Theophilus Pierce Crutcher (1829–1898). Dr. Crutcher and his wife, the former Julia Bidwell, lived at 834 Lichey Avenue. They had six children. A great granddaughter, Sarah Alelaide Shull, married W. Lipscomb Davis Sr., whose company, Davis Cabinet Company, was on Crutcher Street at the corner of South Fifth Street for many years in the twentieth century. *See Lischey Avenue* and *Wilburn Street.*

CUMBERLAND HILLS DRIVE. *See Mansker Drive.*

CURREY ROAD, in the Glencliff area, was named for the family of Robert Brownlee Currey, who was both postmaster and mayor of Nashville in its early days. Currey's son, Dr. R. O. Currey, state geologist, minister, and physician, lived on Currey Hill, later called Rock Crusher Hill. The high ground is now the site of Rose Park.

DANBY DRIVE begins at Elysian Fields Road and goes south, crossing Harding Place and Blackman Road before ending at Briarwood. Robert T. "Bob" Coleman and his father, Samuel F. Coleman, named the street in their development for a friend named Dan.

DANYACREST DRIVE runs east off of Lebanon Pike in Clover Bottom. The street was named for Danya Kendall by her stepfather, Henry Atkeison (who was in the city Codes Department) about the time she married Dr. William L. Downey in 1960. *See Downeymeade.*

DAVIDSON ROAD extends east from US Highway 70 to Harding Road. It is named for the Davidson family, one member of which, Samuel Brown Davidson (1802–73), lived on Charlotte Pike seven miles from town. His plantation included land on Fletcher's Creek in the vicinity of present-day Davidson Road.

DAVIS AVENUE is a one-block-long street located one block east of Gallatin Pike between Leland and Litton Avenues. The avenue was named for Jefferson Davis, president of the Confederate States of America.

**DR. WALTER DAVIS BOULEVARD** skirts the Tennessee State University campus on the north and west. The road begins at Ed Temple Boulevard and goes west to end at Fifty-First Avenue North. The street was named for the president of Tennessee A & I University from 1943 to 1968.

**DEADERICK STREET** goes downhill from Sixth Avenue North to the public square. The street was named for George M. Deaderick, Nashville's first banker. In the 1880s, Deaderick was one of the city's best-known streets. Only two blocks long and about eighteen feet from curb to curb at the time, it was busy and crowded. Gambling houses thrived on the street. A favorite place for farmers to gather was at Harry Adam's saloon, called the Countryman's Delight. As a boy, my father, Jesse Wills (who was born in 1899), enjoyed watching the horse-driven fire engine charge out of the fire station on Deaderick Street.

**DEER PARK** is the name for both a "circle" and a "drive" in Belle Meade. General W. G. Harding's Deer Park occupied this area until the Civil War. The lots between Jackson Boulevard on the east and Deer Park Drive on the west, including Deer Park Circle, show on A. M. Bransford's subdivision plan in the plat that was recorded on August 23, 1919.

**DEMONBREUN STREET**, in downtown Nashville, was named for Timothe Demonbreun, a French-Canadian fur trader, officer in the Revolution, and the lieutenant governor of the Illinois Territory. Demonbreun lived in a cave on the east bank of the Cumberland River between Mill Creek and Stones River for several winters before the Cumberland settlement was established in 1780.

**DEMOSS ROAD** is a short street near the WSMV television tower west of White Bridge Road. The street was named for a prominent nineteenth-century family in Davidson County. A number of Demoss descendants still live in West Nashville.

**DEMPSEY DRIVE** is between Seven Oaks Park and the Nashville International Airport. It occupies land formerly owned by Mr. and Mrs. Dempsey Weaver, who lived at Kingsley (a palatial home designed by William Strickland) in the mid and latter part of the nineteenth century.

**DEW STREET**, between South Sixth and South Seventh Streets in East Nashville, was developed in 1891. The street was named for J. H. Dew, who owned and subdivided the property.

**DICKERSON PIKE** (US 41 and 31 West) begins near Interstate 65, exit 85, in lower East Nashville. It heads north, crossing Old Hickory Boulevard, and continues on to Goodlettsville. North of there, US 41/State Highway 11 goes on to Springfield, while US 31 West heads to Bowling Green, Kentucky (passing through Franklin, Kentucky). Dickerson Pike was named for the Dickinson Meeting House, built by Jacob McGavock and other members of the Primitive Baptist Church. The name Dickinson Meeting House Road was, in time, abbreviated to Dickerson Road. The road was later known as the Louisville and Nashville Turnpike Road.

**DIVISION STREET** is an important connector street between Music Row and Eighth Avenue South. In 1910, the street was the dividing line between the Tenth and Eleventh Civil Districts.

**DIXIE HIGHWAY** was conceived by auto enthusiast and promoter Carl G. Fisher in about 1914. In April of that year, a group of governors from seven states met in Chattanooga to map out the road that would go from Mackinaw City, Michigan, to Miami, Florida. They agreed that the highway should be called the Dixie Highway and that it would have two routes, a western route through Chicago, Indianapolis, Louisville, Bowling Green, and Nashville to Chattanooga where it would join the eastern route that would come down through Toledo, Cincinnati, Lexington, and Knoxville to Chattanooga (the headquarters of the Dixie Highway Association from 1915 to 1927). From Chattanooga, Dixie Highway would continue south through Atlanta to Florida.

Despite a great deal of publicity, the road was exceedingly slow to materialize. In 1915, Dixie Highway boosters from Nashville drove to Cave City, Kentucky, via Gallatin, Scottsville and Glasgow, before returning through Bowling Green, Franklin, and Springfield. Along the route, rallies were held and speeches made to drum up interest. At Franklin, boosters put up a streamer across the public square that read, "It's a long, long way to Dixie, but Franklin's free mineral water makes this way best."[10]

Slowed by World War I, the Dixie Highway was not completed until 1925. The most difficult section was the Monteagle Mountain pass between Nashville and Chattanooga. Marion Couny sold bonds and began building the road in 1916 but ran out of money when half done. The Tennesee Highway Department finished grading a roadway up the mountain from Kimball in 1918 but rain soon washed deep ditches in the roadbed. Without any maintenance money, the Highway Department did not get back to the project until 1923, when it began regrading and surfacing the road. Two years later, the Dixie Highway snaked up the mountian with a macadam surface rolled in place.

A special committee of the State Senate inspected the work. They reported the road in fine condition and said that they had been able to drive from Nashville to Chattanooga in five and one-half hours. The achievement was considered so important that Monty Farrar, the Highway Department's first public relations director, got Nashville's new, high-powered radion station,

*This photograph of three people beside a Dixie Highway sign (D.H.) was taken 6.5 miles east of Murfreesboro on today's U. S. 41. Such signs were approved at the May 1916 meeting of the Dixie Highway Association in Detroit, Michigan.*

LISA RAMSEY COLLECTION

WSM, to advise tourists that the Monteagle Mountain Road was no longer a dangerous mule trail.

In Davidson County, the Dixie Highway was today's US 31West from Goodlettsville to downtown Nashville and US 41 from downtown to the Rutherford County line. Today, such roads as the Dixie Highway, the Broadway of America (US 70), and the Jackson Highway, linking Chicago with New Orleans, via Nashville, are almost forgotten. Beginning in 1925, the US Government implemented a cohesive national road numbering system that did away with such colorful names.

**DOMINICAN DRIVE** extends east from Buena Vista Park to become Third Avenue North. It was named for the Dominican Motherhouse, built 1860–62, at today's 801 Dominican Drive.

**DONELSON PIKE** connects Murfreesboro Pike and the Nashville Metropolitan Airport with Lebanon Pike in Donelson. Donelson Pike was named for John Donelson, who cofounded Nashville with James Robertson in 1779–80. Cleveland Hall and Tulip Grove are two Donelson family homes in this area.

**DOUBLE DRIVE**. *See Riverside Drive.*

**DOUGLAS AVENUE** begins at Dickerson Road and heads east, emptying into Scott Avenue. It was in the Douglas Levine subdivision recorded on May 6, 1924. In 1928, the western part of Douglas was called Ligon Lane for a resident of the area. Another section, from Lischey Avenue to the railroad tracks at McFerrin Avenue, was called Mile End until the early 1960s.

**DOWNEYMEADE** runs north from Lebanon Pike to a park by Stones River. It was named for Dr. William L. and Danya Downey, about the time they married in 1960. The developer of the Stanford Country Club subdivision, Carl Batson, named another street in the subdivision Jenry Drive, combining parts of the first names of Danya's mother, Jennie, and stepfather, Henry Atkeison. *See Danyacrest Drive.*

**DRAKES BRANCH ROAD** begins at Hydes Ferry Pike and heads north, crossing Drakes Branch Creek numerous times. The road and the creek were named for the Drake family, who lived on the road.

**DR. D. B. TODD JR. BOULEVARD** was called Eighteenth Avenue North until Metro Councilman James Darden and officials from Meharry Medical College successfully petitioned for a name change. On February 2, 1982, the section of Eighteenth between Charlotte Avenue and Clay Street was changed to honor Dr. Todd, who died in 1980 at age forty-eight. He was the first African American cardiovascular surgeon in Nashville and headed the surgical team that performed Meharry's first open-heart surgery in 1972. Todd had been chief of thoracic and cardiovascular surgery at Meharry Medical College.

**DREXEL STREET** is between Seventh and Eighth Avenues South, immediately past the split of Eighth Avenue South and Lafayette Street. It was named for Mother Katherine Drexel, Superior of the Sisters of the Blessed Sacrament, who established a convent and school for work among African Americans in South Nashville early in the twentieth century.

**DRY FORK ROAD**, in northwest Davidson County, has its upper end at the Clarksville Pike. The road follows Dry Fork Creek on its left, south to Buena Vista Pike. In 1871, the road literally used the shallow and often dry creek bed as its roadbed for much of the way to Buena Vista Pike. Hence, the name.

**DUBOIS DRIVE** is between Buena Vista and Whites Creek Pike. The street was named for W. E. B. DuBois, a cofounder of the National Association for the Advancement of Colored People (NAACP) and an aggressive and effective advocate for African American rights.

**DUDLEY AVENUE** runs from Thirty-Second Avenue South to Natchez Trace. The street was named for Dr. William L. Dudley, professor of chemistry, dean of the Vanderbilt medical department, and (from 1895 until his death in 1914) president of the Southern Intercollegiate Athletic Association. Dudley Avenue first appeared in the city directory in 1907.

**DUE WEST AVENUE** runs from Fernbank Street, along the Cumberland River, almost due west to Dickerson Road. Originally, the road ran three miles from the Gallatin Pike to Dickerson Road, and was named Goodrich Road for Mrs. Goodrich, who lived on Gallatin Pike.

Montague subdivision was platted in March 1891. It was bound on the west by Gallatin Pike, on the north by Gibson's Creek, on the east by the Cumberland

River, and on the south by Due West. Montague was named for Montague Ross. The lots on the river's edge were used for summer camp houses by people of means. Boat landings were at the end of Fernbank Drive.

**DUNALIE** is the name for both a "court" and a "drive," southeast of Briley Parkway and northwest of Seven Oaks Park. Dunalie Court and Dunalie Drive are very close to the site of Dun Ailie, the beautiful country place of Mr. and Mrs. Lem R. Campbell. The Campbells lived there early in the twentieth century. The Gaelic name means "Ellen's Hill." Ellen was the name of Mrs. Campbell's mother. The house was built on a hill overlooking Murfreesboro Pike to the east and the Overton Hills to the west.

**DUNBAR DRIVE** is one of many streets between Buena Vista Pike and Whites Creek Pike named for prominent African Americans. Dunbar Drive was named for Lawrence Dunbar (1872–1907), a nationally recognized poet of the late nineteenth and early twentieth centuries.

**DUNHAM SPRINGS ROAD** connects Wilsonia Avenue and Hickory Valley Drive at the Hillwood Country Club. The street was named for someone in the Dunham family, possibly for Daniel A. Dunham, who built Dunham's Station on nearby Richland Creek where the Belle Meade plantation later developed.

**EARLY AVENUE** is a short, L-shaped street that connects Greenwood Avenue on the north and Porter Road to the southeast. The street was named for the John and Willie Evans Fall Early family who lived at their home, Pontotoc, on the corner of Greenwood and Scott Avenues, three and one-half miles from the Nashville Public Square. Initially a summer home, the Earlys lived at Pontotoc full-time by the time their first child, Margaret Evans Early, was born in 1903. Each work-day morning, Mr. Early would ride to town in his buggy pulled by his finest stallion, The Emperor, to a livery stable on First Avenue North. He then would walk to his nearby business, the Early-Mack Company, at 315 Second Avenue North. Early-Mack was the finest harness store in Nashville. It also sold bridles, lap robes, pony buggies, saddles, and all horse goods. He was said to be the last of his friends to purchase an automobile. Mr. Early was president of the Board of Trustees of Montgomery Bell Academy from 1923 until 1930, and served on the Nashville School Board. *See Pontotoc Avenue.*

**EAST BROOKFIELD DRIVE**, which curves from Belle Meade Boulevard to Chickering Road, was developed as part of a forty-four-lot Warner Park subdivision developed by B. E. Woodard in 1946–47. Prior to 1946, there was a triangle-shaped field between Belle Meade Boulevard and Chickering Road north of Percy Warner Park.

**EASTLAND AVENUE** begins at Gallatin Pike and runs east before circling north to end at Greenwood Avenue. *See Vaughn Pike.*

**EATONS CREEK ROAD** begins at the Clarksville Pike and runs south, crossing Little Marrowbone Creek, skirting Beaman Park to the west, and following the course of Eatons Creek south to its end at Hydes Ferry Pike. The creek and the road were named for the Eatons, who were early settlers on the headwaters of Eaton's Creek.

**EDENWOLD ROAD** begins at the Gallatin Pike and runs east to Edgefield Junction Road. In 1910, the Edgefield Junction Post Office was renamed Edenwold Post Office. Edenwold was also the name of Walter O. Parmer's stud farm, where, early in the twentieth century, he had as many as sixty brood mares.

**EDGEFIELD JUNCTION ROAD**, in the Rivergate area, preserves the name of Edgefield, the early name for East Nashville. Governor Neill S. Brown named the area in which he lived Edgefield. The city of Edgefield was incorporated in 1868 and existed until 1880, when it was annexed by Nashville. Edgefield Junction, north of Edgefield, was a village with a post office at the junction of the Louisville & Nashville Railroad and the St. Louis & Southeastern Railroad.

**EDGEHILL AVENUE** runs from Twenty-First Avenue South, across from Vanderbilt University, east to Eighth Avenue South. The street was named for Edgehill, the home of Mr. and Mrs. Charles A. R. Thompson that, until 1911, stood on the corner of Edgehill Avenue and what was then Hillsboro Pike. Mr. Thompson owned a dry-goods business, Thompson & Company, at 213 Fifth Avenue North. In 1911, after Peabody Normal College bought his property, he had his house dismantled and moved to Golf Club Lane, then a gravel road that ran alongside the Nashville Golf and Country Club. The house still stands at 211 Bowling Avenue.

**EDGEWOOD AVENUE**, a short distance from the American Baptist College, may have been named for Edgewood, a mansion built in 1854 by Col. Anthony Wayne Johnson, a capitalist and friend of Andrew Jackson. Edgewood stood at 719 North Twelfth Street until 1962, when it was razed for an eighteen-unit apartment house.

**EDMONSON PIKE** begins at Nolensville Pike across the street from Southern Hills Medical Center. It heads south, crossing Old Hickory Boulevard, to the Williamson County line. Edmonson Pike, formerly called the Owen-Winstead Pike, carries the name of one of Davidson County's families in that area.

**ED TEMPLE BOULEVARD** begins at the Clarksville Highway as a continuation of Rosa L. Parks Boulevard. The road runs south, skirting the east side of the Tennessee State University campus, before ending at Jefferson Street. The boulevard was named for the legendary track coach at Tennessee State University. Known as the trainer of champions, Temple's greatest star was Tigerbelle team member Wilma Rudolph, who won three gold medals at the 1960 summer Olympics in Rome.

**EIGHTEENTH AVENUE** was formerly named Salem Street (south of Buchanan Street), McTyeire, Lamar, and Baxter. These names became obsolete in December 1904, when the streets were combined into Eighteenth Avenues North and South.

**EIGHTH AVENUE** was, prior to December 1904, called Bremen and Spruce Streets. In 1909, Eighth Avenue, between Church and Broadway, was widened by five feet on each side to a width of sixty feet. Before the Board of Public Works project began, one side of the street was paved in vitrified brick while the other side of the street railway had a badly worn bitulithic pavement installed in 1901. After the completion of the project, the street would be completely paved with vitrified brick. Ward's Female Seminary, at 15 South Spruce Street, was an outstanding girls' school. Its founder and president for twenty-two years was Dr. William E. Ward. Six years after Ward's death in 1887, John D. Blanton became president. He served in that capacity until the school merged with Belmont Intercollegiate School to become Ward-Belmont in 1913. Suffragist Ann Dallas (Mrs. Guilford) Dudley and Mrs. John Nance Garner, wife of a United States vice president, attended Ward's Female Seminary. *See Spruce Street.*

NASHVILLE, Tenn.    WARD SEMINARY.

*Ward's Female Seminary was founded in 1865 by Dr. William E. Ward as an exclusive school for young ladies. Located at 15 Spruce Street (Eighth Avenue North) from 1866 to 1913, the school merged with Belmont Intercollegiate School in 1913 to form Ward-Belmont. Courses included Latin, history, French, English, and arithmetic. The house was, in the 1890s, the office of Dr. Giles C. Savage. It is today's Standard Restaurant at 166 Rosa Parks Boulevard.*

RIDLEY WILLS II COLLECTION

ELECTRIC AVENUE is one of several streets that lead into Shelby Park from the west. It was named in recognition of the Tennessee Electric Railroad Company that owned the land on which the road was built.

ELEVENTH AVENUE was known, before December 1904, as Woodward, Tilden, Cumberland, McCreary, and Kayne Avenues (to Stevens Street), and King, Ora, and Koscis Streets.

ELGIN STREET was named for the Elgin National Watch Company, founded in 1864 in Elgin, Illinois. A Nashville jeweler suggested the name.

ELIZABETHAN DRIVE runs from Hillwood Drive to Hickory Valley Road. H. G. Hill Jr., who developed Hillwood Estates, named the street for his sister, Elizabeth Hill Penick.

*This 1968 aerial view of Eighth Avenue South shows Wedgewood Avenue in the lower left corner. The next street running east from Eighth Avenue South is Roycroft Avenue, while the third is Benton Avenue. South Douglas Avenue ends at Douglas Corner on Eighth Avenue, a short distance south of Benton Avenue. Judson Baptist Church, which stood at 2120 Eighth Avenue South until 1969, can be seen on the left side of the street. In the distance is the 100 Oaks Mall, which opened in 1968 at 719 Thompson Lane.*

KERMIT C. STENGEL JR. COLLECTION

**ELKINS AVENUE,** two blocks south of Charlotte, in Sylvan Park, was named for the Elkins family who lived on the 3800 block. Most of the other streets running parallel to Charlotte were named for states.

**ELLINGTON PARKWAY** is a major limited-access parkway that runs from Main Street near Interstates 65 and 24 to become Briarville Road just north of Briley Parkway. The parkway was named for Buford Ellington, a two-time governor of Tennessee (1959–63 and 1967–71).

**ELLISTON PLACE** was named for Joseph T. Elliston, 1814 mayor of Nashville and silversmith, who purchased a 360-acre estate in 1816, where Elliston Place is today. His son, William R. Elliston, erected the mansion, Burlington, in 1850 from plans designed by William Strickland. The house burned in 1931. Today, Elliston Place is a commercial district that extends from Twenty-First Avenue North to West End Avenue.

**ELM HILL PIKE** splits off of Murfreesboro Pike across from Trevecca Nazarene University and runs east, north of Interstate 40 East, before terminating at Bell Road. Elm Hill Pike, when it was still a country road, was called Chicken Pike.

On leaving Murfreesboro Pike on Elm Hill, the first historic site is Mt. Ararat Cemetery on the north side, founded in 1869. In the twentieth century, it was purchased by the owners of Greenwood Cemetery, located about a mile further out the pike. Greenwood Cemetery was established on thirty-seven acres in 1888 by Preston Taylor, an influential African American preacher, undertaker, and businessman.

Buchanan's Station, established by John Buchanan as early as 1784, stood where Elm Hill Pike crosses Mill Creek. In 1792, some five hundred Creek and Cherokee Indians besieged the station but were bravely repulsed by twenty-one settlers. In 1915, Peabody College established the Seaman A. Knapp School of Rural Life on one hundred acres that included the site of Buchanan's Station.

Mud Tavern, built of cedar logs with a mud and stick chimney, is thought to have stood near the intersection of Elm Hill Pike and McGavock Pike. Andrew Jackson often stopped there on his way to Nashville from his home, the Hermitage.

**ELMINGTON AVENUE** extends southeast from West End beside and east of West End Junior High School. The street's first resident was Rev. Alex Lipscomb, editor of the *Gospel Advocate* and president of Lipscomb College. He lived there from about 1915 to 1922. Elmington Place subdivision, between Byron and Richardson Avenues, was developed by Wakefield Davis Realty Company in the mid-1920s. Elmington Avenue was named for Elmington, the estate of Percy Warner. In 1901, the members of the Nashville Golf and Country Club purchased ten acres of the Percy Warner estate where they built their clubhouse.

ELMWOOD AVENUE connects Belmont Boulevard and Granny White Pike. The street was probably named for Elmwood, the W. W. Berry home that stood three miles from town on the Franklin Pike.

ELYSIAN FIELDS ROAD runs east and west from Nolensville Pike to Trousdale Road. It may have been named for Elysian Fields in Hoboken, New Jersey, where the first known baseball game was played under the rules of Abner Doubleday on June 19, 1846.

ENQUIRER AVENUE extends from Leake Avenue to Harding Place in Belle Meade. The street was named for Enquirer, a thoroughbred sire that Gen. W. H. Jackson purchased in 1879 to back up the aging Bonnie Scotland. Enquirer, named for the *Cincinnati Enquirer*, stood at Belle Meade until 1895. In 1928, a large two-story house made of cypress clapboard stood in the middle of Enquirer Avenue for most of the summer. The house, built in about 1916, had stood at 714 Enquirer Avenue until Mr. and Mrs. Marshall Derryberry bought it with the intention of moving it to a lot they owned on Howell Place. Their plans fell apart when the Nashville Street Railroad and Light Company refused to let them cross its electric streetcar track because doing so would cause the company to stop service while they cut power lines. With his house sitting in the street, Mr. Derryberry frantically sought a lot on Enquirer on which to put his house. The only available lot was at the corner of Enquirer and Leake Avenue. Mr. Derryberry bought the lot that faced Enquirer. Realizing that the lot was too narrow to accommodate the house, he dug a basement parallel to Leake Avenue and put the house sidewise, facing that street. The house is today the home of Dr. and Mrs. Angus M. Crook at 407 Leake Avenue. The Crooks purchased the house in 1969. Today, the original site of the house is the garden of Mr. and Mrs. Will T. Cheek on Enquirer.

ENSWORTH AVENUE crosses Woodlawn Boulevard beside Ensworth School. The school was named for the street at the suggestion of Lawrence Dortch, a founding board member. The road, much older than the school, could have been named for Ensworth, the home of Henry Martin Hayes, brother of Adelicia Hayes. Another possibility is that the street was named for the Ensworth Dairy Farm owned by John Goodall, who had married Lera Williams, a granddaughter of Willoughby Williams, an early owner of the land where the road is located.

**ESSEX PLACE**, originally named Josephine Avenue, first appeared in the city directory in 1913. It was carved out of the Edgar Jones estate and was part of the Bransford Realty Company's subdivision, platted in 1912.

**ESTES ROAD** extends south from Woodlawn Boulevard to Harding Place. At Hobbs Road, Estes passes Harpeth Hall School on the west. Harpeth Hall is on the site of the former Pat Mann Estes home. The street was named for Mr. Estes, an attorney, who was one of the founders of Life and Casualty Insurance Company in 1902. The other founders were A. M. Burton, Guilford Dudley, J. C. Franklin, and Lena Haralson. In 1940, the few homeowners on Estes, south of Hobbs, picked up their mail from mailboxes at the corner of Estes and Glen Eden Drive.

**EVELYN AVENUE**, in Belle Meade, was once part of the famed Deer Park at Belle Meade plantation. The street crosses Richland Creek a few yards east of Harding Road. When the creek floods, metal barriers are erected to prevent drivers from trying to ford the creek. Before the barriers were installed, cars occasionally were swept down the creek when drivers ignored the high water. Evelyn Avenue was named for Evelyn Bransford (Mrs. Charles) McVeigh, daughter of Johnson Bransford, whose home, Deerfield, at 210 Evelyn Avenue, was completed in 1915. Evelyn Avenue, along with part of Clarendon Avenue, all of Cornwall Drive, the north side of Sutherland Avenue, and seven lots of the west side of Belle Meade Boulevard, were in a subdivision of part of the home place of Johnson and Anna Mary Bransford. The subdivision plat was recorded on October 26, 1928.

**EWING AVENUE** extends south to the inner loop from Lafayette Street. It was named for Andrew Ewing, the first Davidson County court clerk.

**EWING DRIVE** begins at Knight Road and runs east, crossing Interstates 24 and 65 to become Ewing Lane that ends at Ellington Parkway. Citizens in the Seventeenth and Twenty-First Road Districts petitioned the October 1910 meeting of the Davidson County Quarterly Court to build the road as an extension of Ewing's Chapel Road, from Brick Church Pike to three-eighths of a mile east of Dickerson Pike, where it would connect with an existing road that led to Gallatin Pike. The petition said that the road, to be called Ewing Avenue, would be in the public's benefit, as the nearest east-west road was Trinity Lane, two miles to the south. Ewing Drive, the current name, was named for Capt. Alexander "Devil Alex" Ewing, an early settler of Northwest Davidson County, who served in the Revolutionary War as aide-de-camp to Gen. Nathaniel Green. Ewing built the first brick plantation house in the area.

**FAIRFAX AVENUE** has long served as a link between West End and Hillsboro. Originally named Jones Avenue after Edgar Jones, who lived at Glen Oak, the street first appeared in the 1891 city directory. The name Fairfax surfaced in 1913. In 1928, realtor Rick Burns offered beautiful homesites in Fairfax Place, described as midway between Hillsboro and West End.

**FAIRFIELD AVENUE** is a flat street that runs between Hermitage Avenue and Lafayette Street. It was named for Fairfield, the home of Maj. William B. Lewis that stood at the intersection of present-day Green and Decatur Streets. Lewis, who moved to Nashville in 1809, was an associate and advisor to Gen. Andrew Jackson. In the 1890s, St. Margarete's Hospital was located on Lewis's former large estate.

**FANNING DRIVE** is in the Antioch area between Dowdy Drive and Richards Road. The road was probably named for Tolbert Fanning (1810–1874), an educator and leader in the Restoration movement which attempted to purge the Christian religion of its many denominations. Fanning was a mentor to David Lipscomb.

**FANNY WILLIAMS STREET** lies between Nolensville Pike and Foster Avenue off Whitsett Road. The short street was named for Fannie Williams, who had lived on the street since 1922, when the area was still called Flat Rock. The granddaughter of slaves, this community leader was 107 years old at the time of her death in October 2000.

**FARRELL PARKWAY** crosses Franklin Road and continues southeast to Stillwood Drive. The parkway and Farrell Road to the west were both named for Mr. and Mrs. Herbert Farrell, who lived at Crieve Hall in the 1920s–1940s.

**FATHERLAND STREET**, a principal street in East Nashville, runs from the Cumberland River near downtown to Shelby Park. It is named for Fatherland, the handsome home designed by Adolphus Heiman and built in 1855 by Dr. John Shelby for his daughter, Mrs. John Phelan. Shelby was a surgeon in the Creek War, during which he was wounded and lost his sight in one eye. He was post-master of Nashville from 1849 until 1853, and accumulated considerable wealth, primarily through land deals. In 1857, Shelby chartered Shelby Medical College, which opened in 1858 and continued for three sessions.

Fatherland stood in the center of today's Woodland Street between Second and Third Streets, and was accessible to town via the Fatherland Street Railroad Company. It's horse-drawn cars ran from the public square to about five hundred feet beyond the intersection of Tenth and Fatherland Streets.

Spring Park, on Fatherland Street at Thirteenth Street, was built in 1885, sixteen years before Nashville established a municipal park system. Because it was built by the streetcar line, it was called a trolley park. Spring Park featured a natural rock face with a small spring-fed lake beneath it. On an island in the middle of the lake, elephant ear and castor bean plants were planted, and nearby was a monkey cage. There were also a gazebo, a bandstand, and shady walkways lined with shrubbery and flowers. The valuable land was sold and subdivided in the 1890s.

The East Nashville fire of March 22, 1916, destroyed many Fatherland Street homes as well as Warner School, the second largest public school in the city. The school stood on South Seventh Street between Russell and Fatherland. In 1919, Fatherland became the Florence Crittenton Home for Unwed Mothers. The mansion was demolished in 1952 by the Nashville Housing Authority to make way for the James A. Cayce Housing Development.

The Dixie Tabernacle, a religious revival house at 410 Fatherland Street, was the home of the Grand Ole Opry from 1936 to 1939. In 1946, the Nashville YMCA leased for $1 per year an underused community center the city owned at Tenth and Fatherland. By the summer of 1948, the East Nashville YMCA, housed in the cramped building, had five thousand visits a month by East Nashville boys. Its indefatigable director, Comer Teal, would become an East Nashville institution.

**FIFTEENTH AVENUE** was, before December 1904, known as Stonewall, Bolles, and Southwest Washington Streets. *See Stonewall Street.*

**FIFTH AVENUE** was formerly named Summer Street. William Driver (1803–83) lived at what is today 511 Fifth Avenue South. He moved to Nashville after retiring from his career as a sea captain. Driver brought with him a flag given him in 1831 that he nicknamed "Old Glory," the first known use of the term.

In 1906, Fifth Avenue North, between Church and Union Streets, was Nashville's premier shopping street. That December, strings of Christmas electric lights were strung for the first time on Third, Fourth, and Fifth Avenues.

Nashville's two oldest church buildings, St. Mary's Catholic Church (1847) and The Downtown Presbyterian Church (1851), grace Fifth Avenue North in the heart of downtown. The house at 102 Fifth Avenue South, just below Broadway, is the oldest building in the downtown area. Originally a single-family residence, the two-story house dates back to the 1820s, according to Steve Brown and Vic Hood, whose company, Leatherwood Folk Arts, restored the house in 1983–84. In the basement, they found plaster, nails, and floors from that period, as well as one and one-half feet of river silt and sand, evidence that the Cumberland had reached that area. *See Summer Street.*

**FIRST AVENUE** was initially Water Street because the bold spring that supplied Fort Nashborough was between College and Market Streets. Bored logs were laid in the ground through which the water flowed by gravity under Water Street (and presumably Market Street) to the fort. Later, Water Street's name was changed to Front Street. Other, newer portions of First Avenue were formerly named Rutledge, Maple, and Shafer Streets. Early in the twentieth century, the water pipes under First Avenue downtown were cast iron. *See Front* and *Water Streets.*

**FIRST STREET** came into being in 1906 when a city ordinance specified that streets running north and south in East Nashville were to be changed to numbered streets, beginning at First Street beside the river. The north-south division was at Main Street. North of Main was North First Street, while south of Main was South First Street.

**FISK STREET** runs between Jo Johnston Avenue and Charlotte Avenue. It was named for Gen. Clinton B. Fisk (1828–90), associate commisioner of the Freedmen's Bureau for Tennessee and Kentucky. He made some abandoned US Army barracks (where the railroad gulch is today) available to the American Missionary Association for the creation of Fisk School and donated $30,000 to that endeavor.

**FLORA MAXWELL ROAD** begins at Nolensville Pike just past Southern Hills Medical Center and goes east to Hopewell Drive. The street was named for Flora E. Jordan Maxwell, a community activist and devoted Christian. She was one of the African Americans who brought the school segregation suit against the Nashville public schools in 1955.

**FOGG STREET** begins at Eighth Avenue South and goes east to Ewing Avenue. The street was named for the prominent Fogg family that included Francis B. Fogg and his wife, Mary Middleton Rutledge Fogg. Francis B. Fogg, a distinguished Nashville lawyer and state senator, was described as "prudent, temperate, discreet, charitable."[11] His wife, Mary, the daughter of Septima and Henry Rutledge, was, with her husband and parents, one of the founding members of Christ Episcopal Church in 1830. She and her mother established the House of Industry, a school for destitute girls, and were among the city's most charitable women.

**FORREST AVENUE** begins at Gallatin Pike just north of Five Points and runs east toward Shelby Park. The street, originally spelled "Forest," was one of many theme streets in the area. Nearby were Elm, Grove, Holly, Linn, Magnolia, Plum, Tulip, and Walnut Streets.

**FORSYTHE PLACE** runs from Belle Meade Boulevard to Lynnwood Boulevard. It was named for J. W. Forsythe, who was a partner in the Belle Meade Park Company formed in 1913 to acquire land in Belle Meade.

**FORTLAND DRIVE** begins at Riverside Drive and runs in a gentle curve east and southeast toward Shelby Bottoms Park, where it dead-ends. The road initially follows what was the driveway to Fortland, the country estate of Dr. and Mrs. Rufus E. Fort from 1909 until his death in 1940. On Sunday morning, December 27, 1942, the house burned. At the time, Mrs. Fort was living with her son, Rufus Fort Jr. The 350-acre farm was subdivided after World War II.

**FOSTER HILL,** in Abbottsford, was named for Capt. John A. Foster, CSA, of the Twenty-Ninth Alabama Regiment, who, with his one hundred men, defended Redoubt Number 4 on December 15, 1864, during the Battle of Nashville. There is a historic marker where Redoubt Number 4 was located in Abbottsford.

**Foster Street** crosses Meridian Street and Lishey Avenue in East Nashville. In January 1859, William L. Foster recorded a plat to develop 104 lots on Foster, Lishey, and Gallatin Pike (now Main Street).

**Fourth Avenue** was, before December 1904, named Cherry Street. Today, Fourth Avenue South becomes Nolensville Pike (US 31-A and 41-A) at the Tennessee State Fairgrounds. In the 1850s and 1860s, the section of Cherry Street between Church and Broad was the home of some of Nashville's most prominent people. The Eastman family lived at 154, Ben S. Weller lived at 136, and John K. Hume lived at 138. William Walker, "the gray-eyed man of destiny,"[12] grew up at the corner of Cherry and Cumberland Alley. This lawyer, journalist, and adventurer became president of the Republic of Nicaragua in 1856 and ruled until 1857, when he was overthrown by a coalition of Central American armies. He was executed by the Honduras government in 1860. Adelicia Acklen lived on the block for many years, as did Capt. William Stockell, whose home was on the west side at 119 Cherry Street, just north of Broad. Dr. Felix Robertson lived in a house at 129 Cherry Street.

At Cherry and Church Streets, the 240-room Maxwell House Hotel stood preeminent from its opening in 1869 until September 17, 1910, when it was eclipsed by the city's first modern hotel, the Hermitage. The ladies' entrance to the Maxwell House was on Church Street because respectable ladies would not set foot on Cherry Street, where men ate, drank, and gambled in the "Men's Quarter."

In South Nashville, Fourth Avenue South passes City Cemetery, established in 1822, between Oak and Chestnut Streets. Among the more than twenty thousand people buried here are Gen. James Robertson, Gov. William Carroll, Brig. Gen. Felix Zollicoffer, and Capt. William Driver.

Sulphur Dell baseball park was located on Fourth Avenue North at Jackson Street. The first night baseball game in Nashville played with permanent lights was held at Sulphur Dell on May 18, 1931. That night, the Mobile Marines beat the Nashville Vols 8 to 1. In 1963, when the last professional baseball game was played there, Sulphur Dell was recognized as being the oldest baseball park in America. Professional baseball was first played there in 1885. Even earlier, the playing field was known as Athletic Park. On Thanksgiving Day 1885, the Nashville Athletic Club football team played the Nashville Football Club at the Athletic Park in the first game of football played south of the Ohio River. *See Cherry Street.*

*This July 1922 photograph shows workmen demolishing the Harry D. Nichol home at the corner of Fourth Avenue North and Union Street that was built by William Nichol in 1819. The work was done to make way for the eight-story Harry Nichol Building at 400 Union Street, built by Caldwell and Company in 1923. Across the street is a corner of the First American National Bank that opened in 1921. Further north on Fourth Avenue is the six-story Vanderbilt Building that once housed the Vanderbilt Dentistry and Law Schools. Notice the policeman's booth in the middle of Union Street.*

KERMIT C. STENGEL JR. COLLECTION

**FRANCIS STREET** turns off Whites Creek Pike to the northeast of West Trinity Lane. The street was named for Francis Cleveland, son of President Grover Cleveland.

**FRANKLIN PIKE** (US Highway 31) received its name because it led to Franklin, Tennessee. The original road south to the Williamson County line was ordered

*This 2011 photograph of a nineteenth-century road at Glen Leven Farm looks south toward Franklin. Historic Glen Leven is on the east side of Franklin Pike, four miles from downtown Nashville. The Thompson family lived there for more than two hundred years before the farm was bequeathed to the Land Trust for Tennessee by Miss Susan West in 2006. The now-abandoned road may have been part of the Jackson Military Road that Andrew Jackson's soldiers built between Nashville and New Orleans between 1816 and 1819.*

LAND TRUST FOR TENNESSEE COLLECTION

to be laid out at the April 1802 meeting of the Davidson County Court. Its path generally followed an old buffalo trail that led from the south to the salt lick near Fort Nashborough. Franklin Pike was a continuation of Spruce Street (Eighth Avenue South). Near the edge of town, it skirted three hills, St. Cloud Hill (Ft. Negley) to the east, Currey's Hill (Rose Park) to the west, and a short distance further, McCampbell's Hill (Reservoir) close to the road to the west. The road then proceeded through the valley drained by Brown's Creek, on the south side of which were the Overton Hills, often called the knobs.

The Franklin Turnpike Company, the oldest in Davidson County, was chartered in 1829 and ground was broken on August 16, 1830. The road was financed

*This 1966 photograph shows a long stretch of Franklin Pike and the Harding Place exchange of Interstate 65. Cheek House and a large portion of the front lawn at First Presbyterian Church are visible on the extreme left, while John Overton High School and its football stadium are also shown. Franklin Road Academy isn't in this photograph as it was not founded until 1970.*

KERMIT C. STENGEL JR. COLLECTION

by four tollgates. Because the prominent Overton and Thompson families at Travelers Rest and Glen Leven were Presbyterians, people sometimes jokingly called the Franklin Pike "the Presbyterian Pike." A "Free the Turnpikes" movement, started in 1895, bore fruit in February 1902, when the Franklin Turnpike Company became the last such company in Davidson County to sell its tollgate turnpike to the county. The selling price was $13,500.

On May 1, 1909, the Nashville-Franklin Interurban Railroad ran its first cars from Nashville's transfer station to the Franklin public square. Much of its track ran along Franklin Pike. A state highways map of designated trunk lines, published by the Department of Highways and Public Works in 1934, showed

Franklin Pike as part of Highway No. 6 that ran from the Alabama state line at St. Joseph to the Kentucky state line above Westmoreland. When my wife, Irene Jackson Wills, was growing up on Norwood Drive in the 1950s, her favorite place in the neighborhood was the Chocolate Shop in the Melrose area. The Chocolate Shop had great milkshakes and curb service.

**FRANSWORTH DRIVE** crosses Post Road and dead-ends between Richland Creek and Harding Pike. Fransworth was originally a private road in the side yard of Mr. and Mrs. Wentworth Caldwell. Mrs. Caldwell decided to make it a public road because so many people used it as an access to Richland Creek, where they fished below and above the dam built by Horace Greeley "H. G." Hill Sr. The street was named for the Caldwells, Frances and Wentworth.

**FREDERICKSBURG DRIVE**, in Forest Hills, south of Tyne Boulevard, was named by developers Karl Haury and Reese Smith Jr. in the 1960s for the Civil War battle in Fredericksburg, Virginia. Fought in December 1862, it was a Confederate victory.

**FREE SILVER ROAD**, less than one-half mile long, connects Whites Creek Pike with West Trinity Lane. It crosses a subdivision of the same name developed by realtor J. B. Haynie in 1898. Free Silver was an important policy issue in the United States in the late nineteenth century. Its advocates, called "Silverites," were in favor of the free coinage of silver. Primarily, they were farmers from the Midwest and South, and miners from the West. As debtors, they would benefit from inflation. Businessmen, primarily in the financial establishments in the East, were opposed to free-silver, as they were creditors who would be hurt by inflation. In the presidential election of 1896, William Jennings Bryan ran on a free-silver platform against William McKinley and lost. Although Bryan's loss took most of the steam out of the free-silver movement, Haynie was, obviously, still a believer.

**FRONT STREET**, now First Avenue, was given that name because the street fronted the Cumberland River. The land between the street and the river was not within the two hundred acres laid out for the town by Thomas Molloy in 1784. At that time, Front Street was called Water Street. In December 1904, the street's name was changed from Front Street to First Avenue, North and South. *See First Avenue* and *Water Street*.

GALE LANE parallels Interstate 440 between Granny White Pike and Franklin Pike. The street was likely to have been named for Dr. Thomas Gale, of Mississippi, who purchased land in the area in 1835, or for some member of his family.

GALLATIN PIKE (US 31 East) started as the Nashville and Gallatin Pike, chartered in 1830. It was over this highway that Gen. Andrew Jackson began his journeys to and from Washington. The road generally follows the route of the road that led from Fort Nashborough to Mansker's Station in present-day Goodlettsville. The pike was a toll road until Davidson County purchased it for $30,000 in 1902 and made the road free to the public. Nashville attorney and congressman John Wesley Gaines spoke of the poor condition of Gallatin Pike in March 1908:

> I went out toward the cemetery [National Cemetery] one moonlight night with some friends of mine in an automobile not long ago, and it was a dangerous ride on that pike because, with the dust flying, we could not see, and many times I had to stop to pass countrymen coming in with their wagons; the teams did not scare either. The roadway needs to be widened. . . . The pike is very narrow; the part that the wagon drives over is not as wide as it should be to make it safe day or night, and there are deep ravines where, if a wagon should go off one side or the other, it would go a great distance down in the bottom down in a creek or branch.[13]

Spring Hill Cemetery, at 5110 Gallatin Pike, got its start after Rev. Thomas B. Craighead became the first Presbyterian minister in the Cumberland Country (an early name for settlements along the Cumberland River). He erected a small stone schoolhouse in Haysborough, a station about five miles from the bluff, on the trace to Mansker's Station. There, he taught school during the week and preached on Sundays. In 1786, this became the first Presbyterian Church in what was then West Tennessee. The school was known as Davidson Academy. In 1801, the academy moved to its own land "on the hill immediately above Nashville"[14] (later known as Rutledge Hill) and near the road leading to Buchanan's Mill. The school became Cumberland College in 1806 and the University of Nashville in 1825.

In the mid-1790s, Craighead is thought to have built a two-story, log house that was covered in clapboard and had its dog-trot enclosed early in the

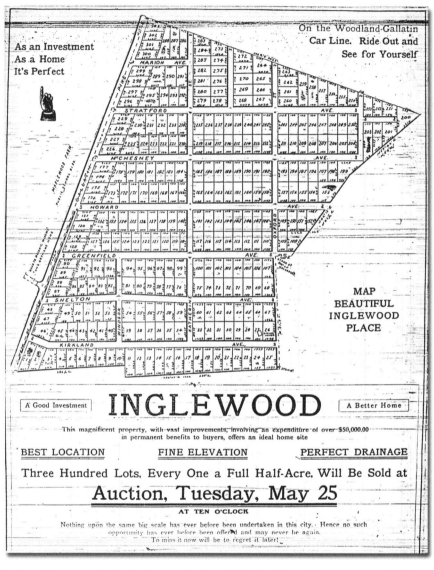

*In the early 1900s, electric streetcar service brought Nashvillians into easy access to Inglewood Place (shown on this 1909 advertisement) and other streetcar suburbs. The Woodland–Gallatin Car Line ran on the Gallatin Turnpike, with stops every other block in Inglewood Place.*

"AUCTION SALE AT INGLEWOOD," *NASHVILLE AMERICAN*, MAY 23, 1909 nineteenth century. The house, Evergreen Place, survived on Gallatin Pike until 2005, when it was razed to make way for a home-improvement store.

Today, the Nashville Auto Diesel College is located on the north side of Gallatin Pike in what was once the summer home of James C. Warner, one of the founders of the Tennessee Coal, Iron and Railroad Company. Upon Warner's death in 1895, Renraw became the home of his son, Percy Warner, who lived there until 1915, when he sold the property and moved to Royal Oaks on Harding Pike. (Renraw is Warner spelled backwards.)

In the 1950s, the Inglewood theater at 3409 Gallatin Pike was popular with local teenagers. The Nashville YMCA built a new East Nashville Branch at 4401 Gallatin Pike in 1961–62. Under Comer Teal's leadership, it became a magnet for high school students in the area.

GARLAND AVENUE formed the southern boundary of Vanderbilt University in 1887. It then ran east from Hillsboro Turnpike to Brown's Avenue. Today, it is a short street between Twenty-Fifth Avenue North and Langford Auditorium. The street was named for Landon Cabell Garland, the first chancellor of Vanderbilt University (1875–93).

GATEWAY LANE connects with Granny White Pike on the west and Lealand Lane on the east. It's name came from its close proximity to the gateway to Lealand, the home of Mr. and Mrs. Overton Lea, on Granny White Pike.

GAY STREET was laid out in 1784 to run from Cherry Street (now Fourth Avenue North) to the western corporate limits. An 1854 map shows it and Line Street (now Jo Johnston), both extending one block further west to McLemore Street and two blocks further east to Water Street. Because Gay Street was in the red-light district immediately behind the State Capitol, it was appropriately named. The street still exists.

GENERAL BATE DRIVE, in Oak Hill, was named by Nashville historian Stanley Horn for Maj. Gen. William Brimage Bate, CSA, who participated in all the major engagements of the Army of Tennessee and who was both governor of Tennessee and a US senator from Tennessee, a position he held at the time of his death in 1905.

*This 1940s view looks northeast from the Gay Street vicinity to, from left to right, the Tennessee Supreme Court Building, the Memorial Hotel, and the National Life and Accident Insurance Company, all on Seventh Avenue North. On the right is the First Baptist Church Capitol Hill, which was the headquarters for the African American students who participated in the lunch counter "sit-ins" of 1960.*

Tennessee State Library and Archives

**GENERAL FORREST** is the name for a "circle," "court," "drive," and "place" named for Confederate Cavalry Gen. Nathan Bedford Forrest, a native of Marshall County, Tennessee.

**GENERAL GEORGE PATTON ROAD**, in Bellevue, was named for Gen. George Patton Jr., who won fame in World War II as commander of the American Third Army. During the Battle of the Bulge, Patton moved his army one hundred miles in forty-eight hours to relieve American soldiers trapped at Bastogne, Belgium.

**GENERAL LOWERY DRIVE** is a short street that enters Harding Place from the south. It is named for Gen. Mark Perrin Lowery, CSA, whose soldiers defended this site during the Battle of Nashville in December 1864.

**GEORGIAN PLACE**, in Belle Meade, was developed in 1959 by George T. Hicks and James Gillespie.

**GEORGE L. DAVIS BOULEVARD** is a stretch of Thirteenth Avenue from Jo Johnston to McGavock Street. It is named for Bishop George L. Davis, the minister of Faith Christian Center in Jacksonville, Florida. Bishop Davis has achieved a worldwide audience through a nationwide weekly radio broadcast; his book, *Lord, Save Me From Me*; and international travel.

**GERALD PLACE** starts at Belle Meade Boulevard and goes to Jackson Boulevard. It was named for Gerald Howard, a friend of Luke Lea.

**GERALD STREET**, west of Dickerson Pike, was also named for Gerald Howard, who developed a subdivision there.

**GLENCLIFF ROAD** runs from Thompson Lane south to McCall Street. It was named for Glencliff, the home built by Major Goff in 1852 on the Murfreesboro Pike, four miles from town.

**GLENDALE LANE** starts at Granny White Pike and runs east to Curtiswood Lane. Four streets in that vicinity have "glen" as part of their name, and four have "dale."

**GLEN ECHO** stretches from Hillsboro Pike in Green Hills to Belmont Boulevard across from the David Lipscomb University campus. The name is the same as the home of early Presbyterian minister, Thomas Brown Craighead, who built a house across from the Spring Hill Meeting House in 1794. The house was destroyed by fire and was rebuilt on a nearby Indian mound in 1810. Emily Donelson Walton, a great granddaughter of John Donelson, named the house Glen Echo when she owned it in 1871.

**GLEN LEVEN LANE** dead-ends into Franklin Pike directly across from Glen Leven, the home of the Thompson family, for which the lane was named.

**GLENROSE AVENUE** begins at Nolensville Pike and runs east and southeast to Thompson Lane. It was named for G. P. Rose, who owned property on Nolensville Pike in 1925 when the Allison subdivision was built along Glenrose.

**GOLF CLUB LANE** runs east from Bowling Avenue, crosses Hillsboro Pike, and then curves to the south, ending at Woodmont Boulevard. Its name makes sense only when you realize that its western terminus originally started at Harding Road beside the Nashville Golf and Country Club and ran south beside the ninth fairway of the golf course. In 1916, the club moved to the Highlands of Belle Meade and, in 1921, changed its name to the Belle Meade Country Club. In about 1937, a decision was made to change the name of the portion of Golf Club Lane nearest the site of the golf course to Bowling Avenue, a move that infuriated Nashville historian Stanley Horn, who did not want his address changed. (Mr. Horn lost that fight.) *See Bowling Avenue.*

**GOLF STREET**, in Inglewood, was named for the East Nashville Golf Club, chartered in 1919, and later renamed Inglewood Golf Club. In 1933, the clubhouse was moved to the corner of Stratford and Shelton Avenues.

**GOWER ROAD** runs south from River Road to Old Charlotte Pike. It was named for the pioneer Gower family. A North Carolina land grant dated November 6, 1784, deeded 640 acres of land to Elijah, Elisha, and William Gower on the south side of the Cumberland River about four miles below the mouth of Overall Creek.

**GRANDVIEW AVENUE**, close to the Interstate 440 exit for Nolensville Pike, was developed as part of the Grandview Heights subdivision. Sale of the lots began in 1900. The name came from the view from the hill on which the lots were developed.

**GRANNY WHITE PIKE** officially begins at Edgewood Avenue. From there to downtown Nashville, the street is Twelfth Avenue South. Until the middle of the nineteenth century, Granny White Pike was called the Middle Franklin

Turnpike because it lay between the Franklin Pike and Page Road that were once called the Upper and Lower Franklin Pikes. Granny White Pike was named in honor of Lucinda White who in 1803, when she was over seventy years old, purchased fifty acres from Woolsey Warrington on then-named Middle Franklin Turnpike. There, "Granny" White ran a tavern.

Senator Thomas Hart Benton is believed to have immortalized Granny White from the US Senate floor by declaring that her tavern had "the best brandy, the best pancakes, and the cleanest beds of any tavern on the road." Benton traveled the road frequently before he moved to Missouri. In the 1840s, Benton's sister-in-law, Mrs. Jesse Benton, then widowed, lived at Sunnyside, a home on Granny White Pike at Kirkwood Lane. Today, the house is the home of the Metropolitan Historical Commission.

**GRANTLAND AVENUE** parallels Eighth Avenue South between Prentice and Bradford Avenues. The street was named for H. W. Grantland, who was associated with the Waverly Land Company in the late 1880s.

**GREELEY DRIVE**, in the Hillwood section of Nashville, was built after World War II. H. G. Hill Jr. named the street for Horace Greeley, whose *New York*

*This photograph, taken about 1910, is of a short stretch of Granny White Pike, south of Otter Creek Road, where "Granny White" had her famous tavern.*

MRS. JAMES E. CALDWELL, COMPILER,
*BEAUTIFUL AND HISTORICAL HOMES IN AND NEAR NASHVILLE, TENNESSEE*

*Tribune* was considered America's most influential newspaper from the 1840s to the 1870s.

GREENFIELD AVENUE, in East Nashville, was developed as part of P. A. Shelton's Inglewood Place subdivision in 1909. Residents in the development, that stretched for seven blocks on the east side of the Gallatin Pike, caught the Woodland-Gallatin Car Line to go downtown. To turn the streetcar around at the end of the line, the conductor would pull down the connector to the electricity, then push up the connector at the other end of the car. He would then move his coin box to the other side, and start back to town. Shelton Inglewood Land Company, that developed Inglewood Place, invited potential buyers in May 1909 to inspect the beautiful homesites, shade trees, concrete sidewalks, rich grass, macadam streets, and lovely surroundings and to come back to the auction of three hundred lots on May 25, each one a full half-acre. The developer bragged, "Nothing upon the same big scale has ever been undertaken in this city."[15]

GREENWOOD AVENUE runs east from Gallatin Pike to Roberta Street, east of Riverside Drive. When Mr. and Mrs. Henry Howe lived on the street, Greenwood was far from town and featured handsome hardwood trees. Mrs. Howe had a lovely wildflower garden that she bequeathed to Cheekwood. It is still called the Howe Wildflower Garden.

GROVER STREET is off Whites Creek Pike beyond West Trinity Lane. It was named for President Grover Cleveland.

GRUNDY STREET runs between Eleventh and Thirteenth Avenues North and between Fourteenth and Sixteenth Avenues North. The street was named for Felix Grundy, one of the most famous lawyers Tennessee ever produced. He served in Congress and in the Tennessee State Legislature, and was a US senator at the time of his death in 1840.

GUN CLUB ROAD connects Post Road with Sedberry Road in West Meade. It was named for the Nashville Gun Club that was there until about 1948. Earlier, there was a Belle Meade Gun Club, with a lodge, on the Belle Meade Farm. In October 1898, there was held, according to the *Nashville American*, "the greatest shooting tournament that has ever, perhaps, occurred south of the Ohio River" at the Belle Meade Gun Club.[16]

HADLEY AVENUE, in Old Hickory, was named for Dr. John Livingston Hadley, one of the largest landowners in what was then Jones' Bend. He purchased 1,171 acres there in 1826. His plantation house, Vaucluse, named for a valley in southern France famous for its association with Petrarch, was on the future site of Dupont's Desulphuring Plant Number 1. In 1896, the name of the bend was changed from Jones' Bend to Hadley's Bend in honor of the Hadley family. Hadley Bend Boulevard, in Lakewood, also honors Hadley's Bend and Dr. Hadley, whose home was demolished in 1924.

HAMPTON AVENUE extends from Bowling Avenue to Hillsboro Pike. It runs through the 122-acre estate purchased by capitalist E. L. Hampton in 1912, from real estate operator W. S. H. Armistead. The property, earlier the home place of brick-maker Samuel Watkins, faced the Hillsboro Pike for more than a quarter of a mile. Its northern boundary was Golf Club Road (now Golf Club Lane), along which it ran for more than four thousand feet. Bordered on the west by what was known as Hillsboro Heights, the property had a fine stand of blue-grass and beautiful hardwood trees. The southern boundary was along the future path of Concrete Boulevard (now Woodmont Boulevard) built by Hampton, W. H. Armistead, and G. A. Puryear in 1914.

Hampton's property also had a large pasture about one block west of Hillsboro Pike that became Nashville's first airfield when transient airplanes began landing there during World War I. Hampton Field ran east-west and was about two thousand feet long. It continued operating, primarily for barn-stormers flying Jennies or DH-4s, for about five years, until the 1921 opening of Blackwood Field on Shute Lane, adjacent to the Hermitage. After that, Hampton Avenue, named for E. L. Hampton, was built and subsequently subdivided.

HARDING PLACE originally extended from Jackson Boulevard to Westview Avenue. By 2011, it stretched from Harding Road to Ezell Road, east of Interstate 65. One of the roads incorporated into Harding Place was Battery Lane, that ran from Granny White Pike to the Franklin Pike in the 1940s. Harding Place was named for the Harding family at Belle Meade. The second oldest house on the street is the residence of Mr. and Mrs. Robert J. Warner Jr. at 4415 Harding Place, designed in 1916 by architect Thomas W. Gardner. During the late 1920s and early 1930s, Mr. and Mrs. Lawrence B. Howard owned the house. According to Sidney Wilkerson, long-time bartender at the Belle Meade Country Club, Mrs. Howard lent the house to a widow named Butterfield. When Mrs. Butterfield went to Michigan during the summers, she normally rented the house. Once, her real estate agent inadvertantantly rented it to a madame who ran a house of prostitution. According to Wilkerson, the police quickly put a stop to that.

**HARDING ROAD,** also called Harding Pike, was, for many years, named Richland Pike for the creek that flowed beside the road. Richland Pike was renamed late in the nineteenth century for the Harding family, owners of the world-famous Belle Meade Plantation. Because the Hardings were members of the Christian Church, Nashvillians sometimes referred to the Harding Pike as "the Christian Pike."

In 1893, Joseph Hayes Acklen, son of Adelicia Acklen, conceived the idea of building a 140-acre gated community on the north side of Harding Pike outside the city limits. At the same time, he built a brick and stone mansion, called Acklen Hall, on the largest plot in what he named West End Park. Acklen and four associates filed a state charter on February 6, 1894, for the development. The original plan called for a broad, tree-lined strip to be left open bordering Harding Pike. Development was slow because of the 1893 financial panic. While some large lots close to Harding Pike sold and handsome houses were built, sales of smaller lots in the rear lagged.

On September 1, 1906, Nashville extended its city limits to expand the city from nine to about sixteen square miles. The city then encompassed Vanderbilt University and West Side Park (now Centennial Park). From that time on, the section of Harding Pike inside the city limits became West End Avenue. In 1909, Acklen sold his interest in West End Park to new investors. The area, now called Acklen Park, still has the tree-lined strip of park land along West End Avenue between Thirty-First Avenue North and Murphy Road.

In 1906, Duncan Dorris drove his white Buick, model 10, over the freshly oiled pike to climb up Nine Mile Hill "in good time." The surface of Harding Pike at that time was macadam. During heavy rains, the surface would nearly wash away. In 1922, state authorities rebuilt the road as a concrete highway from

Park Circle to Belle Meade Boulevard. The road was then twenty-four feet wide with a six-inch deep concrete base.

In 1934, a year after Governor Hill McAlister signed the state law allowing beer to be sold in Davidson County, the Wagon Wheel opened on Harding Road near the Highways 70 and 100 split. It advertised itself as having Nashville's largest dance floor, accommodating five hundred. On opening night,

*This early 1960s view of the Belle Meade Shopping Center shows the Belle Meade Theater facing Harding Road at Ridgefield Drive, a short street that curves behind the theater to end at Woodlawn Drive. Anthony "Tony" Sudekum, who developed the theater, named the street for his home, Ridgefield, visible in the large lot between the theater and the Wellington Arms Apartments at 4125 Harding Road. Immediately west of the shopping center is Gracie's Ladies Shop. Across Harding Road is a two-story brick house that was Jimmy Kelly's restaurant from 1949 until 1982.*

KERMIT C. STENGEL JR. COLLECTION

Jimmy Gallagher's orchestra was featured. By July, bandleader Beasley Smith was broadcasting some of his programs from the Wagon Wheel ballroom over Radio Station WLAC. In 1934 or 1935, when Elizabeth Craig was a teenager, Eddie Dutchin brought his nationally-acclaimed orchestra to the Wagon Wheel. Elizabeth's father, Edwin Craig, allowed her to take several friends to the Wagon Wheel for Dutchin's perfomance. After all, Duchin and his wife spent the night at Mr. and Mrs. Craig's home on Belle Meade Boulevard. That was the first time Elizabeth was allowed to go to the nightclub. For nearly five years, the Wagon Wheel showcased both local and national bands, hosted post-Vanderbilt football game dances, and held dance contests and charity dances.

On July 19, 1939, the Wagon Wheel burned to the ground. It was replaced in 1940 by the Colonial Dinner Club that was located at the split of Highways 70 and 100 across Harding Road from where the Wagon Wheel had been and where the A-1 Appliance Company stands today. Les Woolridge was the manager and owner of the club that temporarily closed in December 1942 because war-time gas rationing made it difficult to attract customers. The club reopened the following October under new management and continued to feature good food and live band music. By November 1945, William O. Daugherty had taken charge as manager. He had previously managed the Belle Meade Country Club from 1941 until 1945. Daugherty advertised the Colonial as having "food cooked right, served right" and with the "South's finest steaks."[17]

One of the club's regular patrons was H. G. Hill Jr., who ate there nearly every night with his girlfriend, Edith Caldwell, whom he would marry in 1961. Later, Daugherty operated the Club Plantation on the Murfreesboro Pike. The Copia was the next club to open at the split of Highways 70 and 100. Also on the north side of Harding Road, it was run by Mike Rose. Ann Byrne Roberts enjoyed going there and to the Lodge, across the highway, in the triangle, when she was Vanderbilt homecoming queen in 1946. Because the Lodge didn't have a cover charge, she went there more often. The Copia food was good, according to Ann Byrne, but she felt the environment left something to be desired. There was a blind piano player there named Sonny. Everyone would stand around the piano, tapping along with his music. In the 1940s and 1950s, George C. Leffler ran Sherries, an upscale restaurant on Harding Road where the Belle Meade Shopping Center is today. Sherries' entrees were usually fried chicken, country ham, and T-Bone steaks. *See Richland Turnpike.*

**HARRISON STREET**, in north Nashville, was named for William Henry Harrison, the ninth president of the United States.

**HAYES STREET** extends from Fifteenth Avenue North to Louise Avenue. It was named for Oliver Bliss Hayes, a prominent Nashville attorney, who died in Nashville in 1858. His oldest daughter was Adelicia Hayes (1817–87), who had married three times and was residing at Belmont Mansion when she was married to Joseph A. S. Acklen and, later, Dr. William A. Cheatham, who was the most distinguished physician in the city and the former superintendent of the Tennessee Hospital for the Insane. In the 1890s and early 1900s, Hayes Street was one of the city's fashionable residential streets. Mr. and Mrs. Adolph B. Hill lived at 1719 Hayes Street. He was in the snuff business. Mr. Hill's wife, Julia Brownlow Hayes, had grown up at her family's home on the northeast corner of Church and Vine Streets, the last of the palatial homes on Church Street to be torn down as the business district expanded to the west. *See Lawrence Avenue.*

**HAYSBORO AVENUE** is a street that empties into Gallatin Pike from the east. It was originally platted in 1923 as Haysboro-on-the-Cumberland, and was made up of cottages for city dwellers who wanted to escape the summer heat. The street was named for Haysborough, a town established on the northern bluff of the Cumberland River a short distance north by the Tennessee General Assembly on October 23, 1799. The town was named for Robert Hayes, brother-in-law of Andrew and Rachel Jackson.

**HAYWOOD LANE**'s western terminus is at Nolensville Pike in the Providence community. The lane, that goes east to Antioch Pike, was named for John Haywood (1762–1826), who, in his thirties, was on the bench of the Superior Courts of Law and Equity in his native North Carolina. In 1807, Haywood moved to Tennessee, where he settled seven miles south of Nashville on his farm, Tusculum, on today's Nolensville Pike. In 1816, this distinguished lawyer became a judge on the Tennessee Supreme Court. He also found time to write *The Natural and Aboriginal History of Tennessee* and became known as the father of Tennessee history. Haywood County, Tennessee, is also named for Judge Haywood.

**HEIMAN STREET** runs from Fourteenth Avenue North to Twenty-Eighth Avenue North. The street was named for Adolphus Heiman, a Potsdam, Prussia native, who moved to Nashville in 1838. An architect, engineer, and builder, Heiman designed and built the main buildings at the University of Nashville and Central State Hospital. He died in 1862, as a result of his imprisonment in a Union jail, and was buried in Confederate Circle at Mount Olivet Cemetery.

**HEMINGWAY DRIVE** parallels Tyne Boulevard one block north. It connects Harpeth Hills Drive and Hillsboro Pike. The street was named for Ernest Hemingway, the Nobel prize–winning novelist and short-story writer, who died in 1961.

**HENRY FORD DRIVE**, in Charlotte Park, was named for the American industrialist Henry Ford, who founded the Ford Motor Company. This was appropriate since the Ford Motor Company built a glass plant in West Nashville in the 1950s. A number of residents in the neighborhood worked there. *See Comet Drive.*

**HERBERT PLACE**, in Belle Meade, was developed in 1959 by George T. Hicks and James Gillespie. Hicks named Herbert Place for his wife's family. His mother-in-law was Sally Herbert.

**HERMITAGE AVENUE** cuts off First Avenue South near where Nashville's General Hospital was before it moved to the renovated George W. Hubbard Hospital in 1999. Hermitage Avenue then passes by Calvary and Mt. Olivet Cemeteries before becoming Lebanon Pike west of its crossing of Brown's Creek. The road was named for Andrew Jackson's home, the Hermitage, toward which it led. Hermitage Avenue was formerly called Fairfield Street, originally named for Fairfield, the home of William B. Lewis, that stood on what was called Lewis Hill (later Rutledge Hill).

**HESTER BEASLEY ROAD** connects Old Harding Pike with Fairview Boulevard just north of the South Harpeth River. The road was named for a preacher named Beasley and a neighbor named Hester, who apparently did not get along.

**HICKORY VALLEY ROAD** extends from Hillwood Boulevard, by the Hillwood Country Club, to Davidson Road. The street was named for the valley in White County, Tennessee, where grocery store magnate H. G. Hill was born.

**HICKS ROAD** runs from just east of Interstate 40 in Bellevue, south, to end at State Highway 100. It was named for Ed Hicks, who lived at Devon Farm just on the other side of Highway 100, where Ensworth School is today. Before the Old Hickory underpass was built, Hicks Road crossed the railroad at Hicks Crossing. There was also a flag railroad stop there early in the twentieth century.

*This view of High Street looks north from near Union Street to the Tennessee State Capitol grounds across Cedar Street. The second house from the right, at 310 North High Street, was occupied by the Elks Club for many years in the twentieth century. The townhouse immediately to its left was the home of Gen. Felix Zollicoffer, CSA, until his death at Fishing Creek, Kentucky, on January 19, 1862. The James K. Polk State Office Building occupies the entire block today.*

ARTWORK OF NASHVILLE, *1894–1901*

HIGHLAND AVENUE was, in the 1930s and 1940s, a residential area convenient to Vanderbilt. Now, it has been shortened to one block between Twenty-Fourth and Twenty-Fifth Avenues South, and is completely within the Vanderbilt campus. *See Jess Neely Drive.*

HIGH STREET, renamed Sixth Avenue in December 1904, was one of Nashville's earliest streets. In the late 1790s, life in Nashville often centered around the sulphur spring. People gathered there knew, from Thomas Molloy's map of Nashville, that a street would go over Cedar Knob (where the State Capitol stands today). As they stood at the spring and looked up, it was obvious that it would be the highest street in the city. When there was enough snow, High Street from Church to Broad was one of Nashville's favorite sledding streets. In the spring of 1866, a bridge, similar to the one on Summer Street, was built on North High Street over Lick Branch. That April, a large sewer on High Street, running south from Spring Street, was under construction, and was "a long-anticipated improvement." *See Sixth Avenue.*

HIGHWAY 100. *See State Highway 100.*

HILLHURST DRIVE is west of Dickerson Road and connects that highway with Ewing Drive slightly to the northwest. The drive was named for Hillhurst, an antebellum home on the Dickerson Pike originally owned by Aeneas Hooper. Hillhurst is no longer there.

HILL PLACE DRIVE is the centerpiece of Hill Place, an exclusive residential development of the H. G. Hill Realty Company in 1995–96. The handsome gated community on the former H. G. Hill Jr. estate fronts on Post Road.

HILLSBORO PIKE (US 431) was named for the Hillsboro community in Williamson County to which it led. In 1809, this road was called the Wharton Road, which forked at Cockrill Spring and was named for Jesse Wharton, who lived in a two-story brick home on the site of Brown's Station (present-day 2306 Golf Club Lane). The name of the town came from Hillsboro, North Carolina, from which many early residents of Williamson County, Tennessee, came.

Tollgate Number 1 on the Nashville and Hillsboro Turnpike, established in 1848, stood just west of today's Blair Boulevard. Initially, the road was to go to

*This view of Hillsboro Pike in the early 1890s shows the road still unpaved. Nevertheless, the presence of a telephone pole indicates progress. As Hillsboro Pike then extended all the way to Grand Avenue. This photograph is likely to have been taken in today's Hillsboro Village, near Belcourt Avenue, looking south toward Blair Boulevard.*

ARTWORK OF NASHVILLE, 1894–1901

the Duck River Ridge beyond Hillsboro, but litigation in the 1880s resulted in shortening the road to twenty-five miles and fixing its southern terminus at the Leiper's Fork (formerly Hillsboro) home where Thomas Hart Benton lived from 1799 until 1815.

In 1901, Davidson County purchased eight miles of the pike and, the next year, Hillsboro became a free pike. By 1910, real estate values along Hillsboro Pike were advancing rapidly, particularly since the pike had been widened to seventy feet and the Hillsboro trolly car line had been built.

In 1925, a Nashville realtor, trying to promote the Hillsboro Pike to affluent prospects, wrote, "There are no factories, no railroads to cross over, no blinding sun while driving in or out of town at any hour of the day [a dig at Harding Pike]. Two of the best motion picture houses in the city are located one and one-half miles on Hillsboro. Very few rental houses, as most all people living there own their own home."[18]

As late as 1935, Hillsboro Pike still led directly to Leiper's Fork. A secondary road cut off Hillsboro just beyond Cartwright's Creek to take traffic to Franklin by Berry's Chapel Church.

*This aerial view of Woodmont Christian Church, 3601 Hillsboro Pike, was taken in about 1947. Woodmont Baptist Church was established in 1942 on Woodmont Boulevard. Its sancuary was not completed until 1956. Notice the absence of a traffic light at the intersection of Hillsboro and Woodmont.*

THE HON. FRANK F. DROWOTA III COLLECTION

HILLWOOD DRIVE, in Nashville's fashionable Hillwood section, was named for the H. G. Hill family, members of which have lived in the area for five generations. In 1936, Ferriss Bailey, an attorney and a good friend of H. G. Hill Jr., bought two lots on the gravel road that Hill's father had recently subdivided. Bailey paid $2,600 for the lots and built his house, designed by Herbert Rogers, at 200 Hillwood Drive. His was the first house built in the subdivision. Two years later, he talked another friend, Francis Craig, the orchestra leader, into building next door at 202 Hillwood Drive. Edwin Keeble designed the Craigs' house that cost $35,000. In 1938, Charles Nelson built a large house at 120 Hillwood Drive, across Post Road from the Baileys. In addition to the homes of two tenant farmers who worked for the Hills, ten families lived on the street by 1941: Mr. and Mrs. Wentworth Caldwell (101), Mr. and Mrs. H. G. Hill (103), Mr. and Mrs. Charles N. Nelson (120), Mr. and Mrs. Ferriss C. Bailey (200), Mr. and Mrs. Garner DeVoe (201), Mr. and Mrs. Francis Craig (202), Mr. and Mrs. Jet Potter (204), Mr. and Mrs. John W. McDougall (228), Dr. and Mrs. Josiah B. Hibbitts Jr. (229), and Mr. and Mrs. Henry H. Miller (231). For the McDougalls, who built their home on a hill at the end of the street, the walk or drive to the mailbox, clustered with the others on Harding Pike at the bottom of Hillwood Drive, was one-mile long. Near the highway, Oman Construction Company had built, during the 1930s, a handsome concrete bridge over Richland Creek and the railroad track. By 1944, mail was delivered to mailboxes at each of the Hillwood Drive homes.

HITT LANE runs from Brick Church Pike to Dickerson Pike, north of Goodlettsville. The lane was named for James Samuel Hitt (1804–69) who, in 1829, moved from Virginia to the land his father-in-law owned between Dry Creek and Mansker Creek. Hitt built a house on a county road that passed immediately in front. The road was later rerouted to its present location but the Hitt family home remained for over 140 years, until it was torn down in 1970.

HOBBS ROAD was named for Billy Hobbs, a beloved farmer who fox hunted in the Seven Hills area and the Little Harpeth River valley. Hobbs Road begins at Hillsboro Pike and runs west to Lynnwood Boulevard, where its name changes to Glen Eden. In 1925, Hobbs Road was sometimes called the Harding-Hillsboro Road.

HOLLY STREET, in East Nashville, runs east from South Eleventh Street to South Twentieth Street at Shelby Park. The Holly Street fire hall, built in 1914, was named for James B. Richardson, a prominent Nashville businessman and philanthropist, who owned the Lockeland Mansion. The fire hall is an East Nashville landmark.

HOLT ROAD connects Edmondson Pike with Nolensville Pike just above the Davidson-Williamson County line. The road was named for some member of the Holt family that settled in the Brentwood area on what is now Crockett

Road. John Holt and his wife, Isabella Hardeman Holt, built a log cabin on their property, where they raised twelve children.

**HOME ROAD** runs between Gallatin Pike and Hart Lane in Inglewood. The street was part of Inglewood's first streetcar suburb, Maplewood Park, that resulted from the chartering of the Maplewood Improvement Company in 1892 by Jere Baxter, J. C. Bradford, and others as a land development company. The year before, Baxter and several partners had chartered the Maplewood Electric Streetcar Company to bring streetcar service from the public square to the Maplewood Farm that Baxter had already purchased. Home Road was named for the Masonic Widows and Orphans Home on Hart Lane, built on land donated by Baxter. The home closed in 1936.

**HONEYWOOD DRIVE**, in Belle Meade, was named for Judge Thomas H. Malone's home, Honeywood, on the Harding Pike next to the celebrated Belle Meade Deer Park. Judge Malone chose that name because of the locust trees that covered the site before his house was built. *See Malone Place.*

**HOOD AVENUE**, in Green Hills, was named for Confederate Gen. John Bell Hood, who commanded the Army of Tennessee during the Nashville campaign of 1864.

**HOOD'S HILL ROAD**, in Green Hills, is also named for Gen. John Bell Hood.

**HOOTEN HOWS ROAD** begins at US Highway 70 South west of Interstate 40 in Bellevue. The dead-end road was named for Squire John Hows and Elder William R. Hooten, whose properties were connected by the road.

**HOPKINS AVENUE** is a short go-between street connecting Woodmont Boulevard and Graybar Lane in Green Hills. The avenue was named for John Hopkins Noel, whose father, Oscar F. Noel, was a friend of Johns Hopkins (1795–1873), the wealthy American entrepreneur for whom Johns Hopkins Hospital and Johns Hopkins University were named.

**HOWELL PLACE** cuts from Belle Meade Boulevard, across Jackson, to the end of the next block, at which point it connects with Iroquois Avenue by a narrow road called Cherokee Circle. Howell Place was named for R. B. C. Howell, the prominent nineteenth-century minister of First Baptist Church.

**HUCKLEBERRY DRIVE**, in Hillwood, runs east from Richfield Drive to Hickory Valley Road. The name Huckleberry is a takeoff on the "Hucklebuckle" game that the children in the H. G. Hill Jr. family played at their summer cottages in Rock Island, Tennessee.

**HUDSON ROAD**, in Neelys Bend, was named for the W. B. Hudson family who farmed in the fertile Neelys Bend.

**HYDES FERRY PIKE** (State Highway 12) runs from Bordeaux to Ashland City. The Hyde's Ferry Turnpike Company was chartered in 1848 to build a road from Nashville to Ashland City and Sycamore Mills. The road was named for Richard Hyde, whose ferry crossed the Cumberland where the railroad bridge

*This view of Hyde's Ferry was taken in the early 1890s, soon after the railroad bridge was built. Richard Hyde ran the ferry which connected North Nashville with Bordeaux.*
ARTWORK OF NASHVILLE, 1894–1901

does today. Business was good until the Hydes Ferry Bridge was built in Bordeaux in 1889. Davidson County purchased its portion of the toll road in 1901 for $10,000. In 1904, residents of the area protested when they learned that a pest house (a hospital used for persons with communicable diseases) would be built on the county farm on Hydes Ferry Pike.

**HYNES STREET** was a narrow side street that ran between Eleventh and Thirteenth Avenues North where the Nashville Electric Service (NES) complex is today. The street was named for Col. Andrew Hynes, who owned a huge warehouse on the street where he stored salt. In 1898, Hynes Street ran from McCreary (now Eleventh Avenue North) to Stonewall Street (now Fifteenth Avenue North) at the old state penitentiary. For many years, Hynes School stood at the corner of Summer (now Fifth Avenue North) and Line Street (now Jo Johnston Avenue). NES conducted a vehicle count on Hynes Street in the 1980s that showed that 98 percent of the traffic was generated by their trucks. As a safety measure, the street was closed to through traffic on December 7, 1987.

**IDLEWILD** is the name for both a "court" and a "drive" in Madison, just south of Neelys Bend Road. They were named for Idlewild, the home of H. B. Chadwell, who subdivided the property in 1914.

**INGLEWOOD** is the name for both a "court" and "drive" that are connecting streets immediately to the east of Gallatin Pike, just south of Briley Parkway. The streets and the Inglewood community were named for the Englewood Forest in the English countryside.

**IROQUOIS AVENUE** begins at Inquirer Avenue, crosses Belle Meade and Lynnwood Boulevards, and ends at Sunnybrook Drive. The street was named for Iroquois, the first American-born and bred stallion to win the English Derby. Iroquois stood at stud at Belle Meade Farm from 1887 to 1899.

**JACKSON BOULEVARD** makes a loop from Harding Pike to Harding Place. Work on the road began on April 10, 1906, with a Nashville firm, Sharpe and Company, as the contractor. The boulevard was named for the William Hicks Jackson family at Belle Meade plantation. In 1911, the speed limit through the deer park on Jackson Boulevard was eight miles an hour.

JACKSON HIGHWAY was a national automobile road connecting Chicago with New Orleans via Nashville. It was named for Gen. Andrew Jackson, the seventh president of the United States. Miss Alma Rittenberry, of Birmingham, Alabama, conceived the idea of the route and its name in 1911. She was a member of the Birmingham Equal Suffrage Association and the United Daughters of the Confederacy. The Jackson Highway approached Nashville on US Highway 31 East from Gallatin. Much as the Jackson Military Road did nearly a century earlier, Jackson Highway went south from Nashville to Franklin on Franklin Pike, and from there to Columbia and Lawrenceburg. It then continued south through Florence and Muscle Shoals, Alabama, before entering Mississippi, where it went through Columbus, Meridian, and Hattiesburg, before ending in New Orleans.

American singer and actress Cher recorded an album, which was a commercial failure, called *3614 Jackson Highway*. It was released in 1969 by ATCO. 3614 Jackson Highway was the address of Muscle Soals Sound Studio in Sheffield, Alabama.

JACKSON MILITARY ROAD was a 516-mile route from Nashville to New Orleans that was proposed by Andrew Jackson as a shorter, more practical route from Nashville to New Orleans than the Natchez Trace. Funded by the federal government, the initial appropriation of $5,000 was announced in 1816. This was followed by an additional appropriation of $5,000 in March 1818. General Jackson was officially in charge of construction of the road that required 75,801 man-days of labor and cost $300,000. The construction crews of from fifty to three hundred soldiers were under the direct supervision, after early 1818, of Maj. Perrin Willis.

The road began in Nashville and went south, likely through land on Brown's Creek owned by Tommy Thompson. A field on Thompson's land where Jackson and his soldiers camped was, for generations, called the "Camp Field" by the Thompson family at their home, Glen Leven. From there, the road went through Franklin, Columbia, and Lawrenceburg before it crossed the Tennessee River on a ferry between Kileen and Florence, Alabama. It then cut cross-country through mostly unoccupied lands of Alabama and Mississippi, including some still owned by the Choctaws. The road still exists in Columbus, Mississippi, where the Jackson Military Road crossed the Tombigbee River. The road then angled down through multiple Mississippi counties before crossing into Louisiana at Pearl River, twenty miles west of Poplarville, Mississippi. It then passed the site of the future town of Bogalousa, Louisiana, to Madisonville, Louisiana, on the north shore of Lake Pontchartrain before making its final descent into New Orleans.

Jackson's military road cut the distance from Nashville to New Orleans by two hundred miles. It declined in importance in the 1840s due to disrepair and its difficult route through Louisiana swamps. It was partially replaced by Robinson Road, that led from Columbus, Mississippi, to Natchez. The Jackson Military Road route later became part of Jackson Highway, established early in the twentieth century.

**JACKSON STREET**, in north Nashville, runs from Second Avenue North west to Dr. D. B. Todd Jr. Boulevard. It is interrupted, however, by the Bicentennial Mall. It was named for Gen. Andrew Jackson, the seventh president of the United States.

**JAMES AVENUE**, in West Nashville, connects Robertson Avenue with Sixty-Third Avenue North. Like Robertson Avenue, James Avenue was named for James Robertson, the pioneer leader of the overland party of settlers in December 1779 who cofounded the settlement that would later be named Nashville.

**JAMES ROBERTSON PARKWAY** was opened in 1957 as an integral part of the Capitol Hill Redevelopment Project that revitalized a slum area north of the State Capitol. The Parkway is named for James Robertson, who cofounded Nashville with John Donelson in 1779–80.

**J. C. NAPIER COURT** runs northwest from Lewis Street, one block north of Lafayette Street. It was named for James C. Napier (1845–1940), who was, between 1872 and 1913, Nashville's most powerful African American politician. A successful businessman and friend of Booker T. Washington, Napier was the first African American to preside over the Nashville City Council. He was a founder and cashier of the One Cent Savings Bank, organized in 1904. Napier's greatest accomplishment was to serve as President William H. Taft's register of the United States Treasury from 1911 to 1913. He was also on the boards of Fisk and Howard Universities.

*This 1962 aerial view of downtown Nashville draws attention to James Robertson Parkway sweeping in a near half-circle around the State Capitol. That year, Nashville's skyline was dominated by the thirty-story Life and Casualty Tower.*

KERMIT C. STENGEL JR. COLLECTION

**JEFFERSON STREET** begins at Hadley Park in north Nashville, near the entrance to Tennessee State University, and runs east to the Jefferson Street Bridge over the Cumberland River. The street, named for US President Thomas Jefferson, is the most important street in Nashville's African American community, thanks in part to its proximity to Fisk University, Meharry Medical College, and Tennessee State University. Before integration, the Ritz Theater on Jefferson Street offered first-run movies. The street also featured barbershops, beauty salons, a hotel near Fisk, and several churches.

Earlier, Jefferson Street and the neighborhood immediately north of it, between the river and Rosa Parks Boulevard, were known as Germantown, named for the German immigrants who lived there after arriving in Nashville in the 1840s and 1850s. Although many German-American families left the area after World War I, this area continues to be called Germantown and has been largely revitalized.

When the settlers first arrived in 1780, they found a large salt lick and sulphur spring that attracted game of all kinds. The spring, called the Great French Lick, was about three hundred yards southwest of the intersection of present-day Jefferson Street and Fifth Avenue North. Kasper Mansker, who had visited the Cumberland Country three times between 1769 and 1775, certainly saw the salt lick. He or another long hunter told James Robertson about the vast herds of buffalo that came there to lick the salt. James Robertson first visited the Great

*The electric streetcar is passing the J. A. Maxey grocery store at 411 Jefferson Street in North Nashville. Advertisements on the streetcar promote professional baseball at nearby Sulphur Dell and a speech on temperance by Edward Ward Carmack at the Ryman Auditorium. This picture was taken early in the 1900s.*

Kermit C. Stengel Jr. Collection

French Lick when he and eight others came to the Cumberland Country in March 1779 to plant corn so that when his party arrived the following December, they would have something to eat. Unfortunately, the crop had been destroyed.

**JESS NEELY DRIVE** begins at Natchez Trace, goes east between Vanderbilt's McGugin Center on the south side, and Dudley Field and Charles Hawkins Field on the north side, to Twenty-Fifth Avenue South. Earlier named Highland Avenue, the street was renamed for Jess Neely, the captain of the undefeated and once-tied 1922 Vanderbilt football team, longtime head football coach at Rice University, and athletic director at Vanderbilt from 1967 to 1973. *See Highland Avenue.*

**JOCELYN HOLLOW ROAD,** in West Meade, stretches in a gentle curve from Davidson Road on its northern end to Brook Hollow Road to the southwest. The road was named for Col. Benjamin Jocelyn, who had a station on Fletcher's

*This Lion gas station stood at the corner of Fifth Avenue North and Jefferson Street in 1950.*
RIDLEY WILLS II COLLECTION

Creek. Harrison Vernon, a man who helped raise me, said that, as a boy in the first decade of the twentieth century, he herded cattle in Jocelyn Hollow.

**JOHN A. MERRITT BOULEVARD** is a continuation of Jefferson Street. It begins beside Hadley Park and runs through the Tennessee State University campus, by the football stadium, and ends between the Student Center and Harned Hall. The street was named for TSU's legendary football coach, John A. Merritt, whose thirty-one-year career record, when he retired in 1983, was 238–67–11.

**JOHN L. DRIVER BOULEVARD** is between Thirty-Seventh and Thirty-Ninth Avenues North on the western side of the Tennessee State University campus. The street was named for a former Nashville city councilman.

**JOHN MALLETTE DRIVE**, in Bordeaux, is between Hydes Ferry Pike and Clarksville Pike. It was named for a biology professor at Tennessee State University who later became part of TSU's administration and an associate chancellor of the Tennessee Board of Regents.

**JO JOHNSTON AVENUE**, in North Nashville, was named for Confederate Gen. Joseph E. Johnston. The street was originally known as Line Street because it was the town's northern boundary line. A part of "Hell's Half Acre," located behind the State Capitol, the street was renamed Jo Johnston Avenue in an effort to distance Line Street from its infamous past and change local perception of the area. *See Line Street.*

**JOY** is the name for both a "circle" and a "street" that are located near the upper end of Lischey Avenue in East Nashville. They were named for the Thomas S. Joy family, who lived on Lischey Avenue and who had greenhouses there for their florist shop that opened on Church Street in 1886.

**KENNER AVENUE** is one block north of Woodmont. It runs from Harding Pike to Estes Road, and honors the name of the Duncan Kenner family that once lived at Woodlawn, a two-story brick house built by John Nichols in 1823. The Kenner Manor subdivision plan for the northern part of the Kenner lands, including forty-one lots on either side of Kenner Avenue, was filed on August 20, 1914. *See Woodlawn Drive.*

**KENNESAW DRIVE**, in Forest Hills, south of Tyne Boulevard, was named by developers Karl Haury and Reese Smith Jr. in the 1960s for the Civil War battle in Kennesaw Mountain, Georgia. Fought from June 19 to July 2, 1864, it was a Confederate victory.

**KENSINGTON PLACE**, on the Vanderbilt University campus, runs from Twenty-Fourth Avenue South, between fraternity houses, including the SAE house on the corner of Kensington and Twenty-Fifth, to dead-end at Natchez Trace. The street was named for the affluent Kensington district of West and Central London within the Royal Borough of Kensington and Chelsea.

**KIMPALONG AVENUE**, which runs behind the campus of Montgomery Bell Academy, was developed in the 1920s as part of the Kimpalong Place subdivision. The origin of its name is unknown.

**KIRKLAND AVENUE** runs from Gallatin Pike to Greenfield Avenue in East Nashville. Unpaved until the 1930s, Kirkland Avenue was a part of the Inglewood Place subdivision developed by the Inglewood Land Company incorporated in 1908. Among its stockholders were H. G. Hill, H. W. Buttorff, and John Early. Kirkland Avenue was named for W. C. Kirkland, another investor in the Inglewood Land Company.

**KIRKLAND PLACE**, named for Vanderbilt Chancellor James H. Kirkland, is deep within the Vanderbilt University campus. The street extends from Twenty-Fifth Avenue South, beside and south of Branscomb Quadrangle, beyond which it circles back to become Twenty-Fourth Avenue South just beyond the University Club.

**KIRKMAN LANE** was originally a narrow wagon road that began at Franklin Pike, climbed part way up a hill, turned north then west, north again, west again, crossing present-day Tyne and Robertson Academy, continued west across Lealand Lane, paralleling the present-day Stonewall Drive, and entered Granny White where Sewanee Road does today. The wagon road was known as Overton Lane and Lea Avenue before becoming Kirkman Lane. It was named for Kate Kirkman, the president of the Women's Department at the Tennessee Centennial Celebration who lived with her husband, Van Leer Kirkman, at Oak

Hill, the mansion Van Leer built on Franklin Pike, where First Presbyterian Church stands today.

**KOREAN VETERANS MEMORIAL BOULEVARD** connects East Nashville with Fourth Avenue South. Its centerpiece is the Korean Veterans Memorial Bridge over the Cumberland River. The bridge opened in May 2004 as the Gateway Bridge to reconnect East Nashville neighborhoods with downtown after the Shelby Street Bridge was closed to vehicle traffic in 1998. In 2003, the Shelby Street Bridge reopened as the city's landmark pedestrian bridge. In 2006, Landmark Bridge and Boulevard were renamed Korean Veterans Memorial Bridge and Boulevard to honor the more than 134,000 Tennesseans who were in military service during the Korean War (1950–53). Korean Veterans Memorial Boulevard is scheduled to be extended to terminate at Eighth Avenue South.

**KREITNER DRIVE** is west of Old Harding Pike in what was originally called the Bellevue Highlands subdivision. The developers named the street for Joseph "Mickey" Kreitner, who formerly owned the property. Kreitner, a Nashville native, was the catcher for the Nashville Vols on their Southern Association championship team in 1943. Called up by the Chicago Cubs at the end of the season, he made his major league debut on September 28, 1943, against the New York Giants at Wrigley Field.

**LAFAYETTE COURT**, across Leake Avenue from the Belle Meade plantation, was subdivided by the Bransford Realty Company as a portion of the Courts of Belle Meade in August 1927. Lafayette Court was most likely named for the Marquis de Lafeyette, the idealistic French nobleman who fought as a major general in the Continental Army and who visited Nashville and Andrew Jackson's home, the Hermitage, in 1825. *See LaSalle* and *Lincoln Courts.*

**LAFAYETTE STREET** (US 41 and 70 South) splits off of Eighth Avenue South and continues southeast to become Murfreesboro Pike before it reaches Spence Lane. Lafayette Street was named for the Marquis de Lafayette.

**LAIRD ROAD** starts at Jocelyn Hollow Road and goes southeast to Post Road in West Meade. The street was named for Becky Laird, who was a friend of H. G. Hill Jr. (the developer of the property), and aunt to Eleanora (Mrs. Neil) Cargile.

*This panoramic view of Lafayette Street, taken in 1946, looks northwest toward downtown. Visible is the Sears Building at 639 Lafayette Street (today's Nashville Rescue Mission) and, in the lower right corner, the old Gallaway Memorial Hospital, which is now a Metro office building housing the Election Commission and other offices at 800 Second Avenue South.*

KERMIT C. STENGEL JR. COLLECTION

**LAKEHURST DRIVE** is a short street in East Nashville just west of Shelby Park Golf Course. The lower half of the street, between Ordway Place and North Twentieth Street, is part of what is known as "Little Hollywood" because the 1930s stucco and Spanish-style houses with tile roofs look as if they belong in Hollywood, not in East Nashville. *See Ordway Place.*

**LANE** is the name for both a "court" and a "drive" located just west of Whites Creek Pike, below that road's intersection with Knight Drive. Both streets were named for Bishop Isaac Lane (1834–1937), a bishop in the Christian Methodist Church and the founder of Lane College in Jackson, Tennessee.

**LASALLE COURT**, across Leake Avenue from the Belle Meade plantation, was subdivided by the Bransford Realty Company as a portion of the Courts of Belle Meade in August 1927. LaSalle Court was most likely named for René-Robert Cavelier, Sieur de LaSalle (1843–87), the North American explorer who claimed the entire Mississippi Valley for France. *See Lafayette* and *Lincoln Courts.*

**LAVERGNE COUCHVILLE PIKE** connects Murfreesboro Pike, less than one mile north of Lavergne, with four Corners Marine Recreational Area on J. Percy Priest Lake. Traditionally, the pike connected Lavergne, in Rutherford County, with Couchville in Davidson County. François Leonard Gregoire de Rouhlac, who came to Rutherford County in 1790 from Limoges, France, named the community where he lived "LaVergne," meaning "the green," because of its grassy meadows and its many cedar trees.

**LAWRENCE AVENUE** runs from Ninth Avenue South to Twelfth Avenue South. The street was named for Corinne Hayes Lawrence, daughter of Oliver Bliss Hayes. She married William Luther Bigelow Hayes in 1855. *See Hayes Street.*

**LEA AVENUE**, between Hermitage Avenue and Fifth Avenue South, was named for Judge John M. Lea, who was president of the Board of Trustees of the University of Nashville for many years. He was also president of the Tennessee Historical Society. The avenue's most interesting house is the Rutledge-Baxter Place, at 101 Lea Avenue. The two-story Italianate residence rests on the site of Rose Hill, the home of Henry and Septima Sexta Rutledge, both of whom were children of signers of the Declaration of Independence. The Rutledge home, noted for its beautiful gardens, was partially burned during the Civil War. When Nathan Baxter built on this site, he incorporated a part of the Rutledge residence that had been built in 1814.

**LEAKE AVENUE** was initially a farm road that separated the stallion barns at Belle Meade Farm from the smaller sheds for the mares that were on the south side of the road. Leake begins at Harding Pike, and runs up the gradual hill to Belle Meade Boulevard. The street was named for J. O. Leake, who lived at Belle Meade mansion from 1909 to 1916.

**LEALAND LANE** was built from Sevier Park to Overton Lea Road in about 1939 or 1940. The lane was named for Lealand, the home of Mr. and Mrs.

*This dirt road at Belle Meade Farm led from the carriage house, shown in the distance, up a slight incline to the east. The frame buildings on the left housed the mares, while the much larger paddocks on the right were for the stallions. This road later became Leake Avenue.*

BELLE MEADE PLANTATION COLLECTION

Overton Lea on the east side of Granny White Pike. Their 1,200 acre farm extended south to Harpeth Hills, where Overton Lea Road is today.

**LEBANON PIKE** (US Highway 70) connects Nashville with Lebanon, Tennessee. Andrew Jackson had a racetrack on the road where some of the finest thoroughbreds of the day raced. The race between Jackson's Truxton and Joseph Erwin's Ploughboy in the fall of 1805 resulted in the duel between Jackson and

Erwin's son-in-law, Charles Dickinson, near Adairville, Kentucky, on May 30, 1806. Clover Bottom Racetrack was in the Stones River bottom on both sides of Lebanon Pike just before today's motorists reach the Stones River Bridge.

The Nashville and Lebanon Turnpike Company was chartered in 1835 to build a road completed two years later. Until 1840, when a bridge was built, users of the road had to cross Stones River on an oar-driven ferry operated by Timothy Dodson, who owned land on the east bank. A highway map of Tennessee showing the designated trunk line system, published by the Department of Highways and Public Works in 1934, showed Lebanon Pike as part of State Highway 24 that ran from its junction with Highway 1 near Nashville through Lebanon to Crossville. This road was also US 70 in 1934. *See Old Lebanon Dirt Road* and *US Highway 70.*

**LEONARD AVENUE** begins at West End and runs south, across Kingfisher Creek, to end at Brighton Road. The street was named for John Leonard Whitworth, who owned a large amount of property in the area.

**LEWIS STREET**, in South Nashville, was named for Maj. William B. Lewis, who lived nearby at his home, Fairfield.

**LINCOLN COURT**, across Leake Avenue from the Belle Meade Plantation, was subdivided by the Bransford Realty Company as a portion of the Courts of Belle Meade in August 1927. Lincoln Court was most likely named for President Abraham Lincoln. *See Lafayette* and *LaSalle Courts.*

**LINCOYA** is the name for both a "court" and a "drive" located in Donelson's Lincoya Hills subdivision. They were named for Andrew Jackson's adopted son, Lincoya, who was from the Creek tribe.

**LINDSLEY AVENUE**, on historic Rutledge Hill, was named for Dr. Philip Lindsley, the distinguished president of Cumberland College. Lindsley renamed the college the University of Nashville in 1826 to eliminate confusion with a newly organized Cumberland College in Princeton, Kentucky.

**LINE STREET** was shown on Thomas Molloy's map of 1784 as the north line of the town. Line Street ran east-west one block north of Gay Street. In the late 1850s, the western part of Line Street was called Bostick Avenue, named for Hardin P. Bostick, who, in a period of financial stress, subdivided his property, creating Bootlick Street. After the Civil War, Line Street directly behind the State Capitol became the center of the red-light district with houses of prostitution lining the street. Citizens living in Germantown were embarrassed about this and would not think about getting off the Line Street and Watkins Park streetcar at the stop in "Hell's Half Acre."

In 1870, Samuel Watkins gave the City of Nashville a rectangular 8.2-acre park, eight or ten blocks west on Line Street. The park, near Watkins's stone quarry, was also bordered by North Addison, Harrison, and Park Streets. Originally called "Watkins Grove," the land had served as an unofficial park in the 1850s. During the Civil War, the Union Army cut the trees in the grove and pastured mules there, ruining it as a park. From then until 1901, when the city chartered its park system, local residents used the area as a pasture and illicit dump. That year, Major E. C. Lewis, one of the five newly appointed park commissioners, inspected the area and decided that, with some work, it could be converted into a respectable park. With a combination of city financing and private contributions, Watkins Park became the first park in Nashville's park system.

Meanwhile, Germantown residents and others convinced the city to change Line Street's tarnished name to Jo Johnston Avenue, honoring Confederate Gen. Joseph E. Johnston. *See Jo Johnston Avenue.*

**LISCHEY AVENUE**, in East Nashville, runs north from Foster Street to East Trinity Lane. The street was named for Louis C. Lischy, a horticulturist whose land faced Lischey Avenue at Douglas Avenue, then known as Mile-End Avenue. Lischy was also a great, great grandfather of Julian Bond, the American social activist, politician, professor, and writer. At Lischy's death, he left his greenhouse glass to his mulatto son, Joseph Browne, who operated a greenhouse and a nursery from 1895 until about 1916.

In 1880, Thomas S. Joy purchased one hundred acres on Lischey Avenue not far north of Lischy's land. There, he cultivated flowers and plants to sell in his retail store on Church Street that opened in 1886.

In 1889, the city council approved an ordinance establishing the Main Street and Lischey Avenue Street Railroad Company to put into operation a street railroad with cars operated by motors run by electricity on what was known as the overhead system.

In 1905, Mr. and Mrs. Theophilus Wilburn Crutcher lived in a house at 832 Lischey Avenue that was still standing in 2011. He operated an insurance agency, Crutcher Brothers, at 832 Fourth Avenue North. The Crutchers were the grandparents of Adelaide Shull Davis, the widow of W. Lipscomb Davis, whose business, Davis Cabinet Company, produced high-quality furniture for many years in the twentieth century. *See Crutcher* and *Wilburn Streets.*

**LITTON AVENUE** begins at Gallatin Pike and runs east to Tammany Drive in the Dalewood area of Inglewood. The street was named for Isaac "Ike" Litton, a businessman well-known to his contemporaries as treasurer of the Missionary Society of the Southern Methodist Episcopal Church. In 1872, Litton and his family lived on a large farm three miles from town on Gallatin Pike.

**LIVINGSTON STREET** is off Fowler Street in Old Hickory. It was named for the family of Robert Livingston, a government diplomat who was given land in Jones Bend as payment for diplomatic services in England.

**LOCKLAND DRIVE**, four blocks west of Shelby Park, was named for Lockeland, a handsome home built in 1810 by Col. Robert Weakley. He named it for his wife, Jane, whose father was Gen. Matthew Locke, of North Carolina. In 1889, prominent Nashville businessman James B. Richardson purchased Lockeland and eight acres. He discovered the curative powers of the spring on his property and began to bottle the water in a small plant on his place. The Louisiana Purchase Exposition of 1904 awarded the Lockeland spring water a grand prize for its "salubrious quality."[19] The Lockeland mansion was purchased by the city in 1939 and torn down in the early 1940s so that Lockeland Elementary School could be built on the site. The Lockeland house faced Woodland Street although an 1870 addition faced South Seventeenth Street.

**LOCK ROAD** begins at Baptist World Center Drive in East Nashville and runs downhill past Seminary Street to dead-end near the river where Eaton's Station was built in 1780. In the 1700s, buffalo forded the river at this point to reach the salt lick on the southern side. Later in the nineteenth century, a ferry crossed the Cumberland here. Lock Number 1 was placed in operation here on November 26, 1904, at a cost of $395,634. Measuring 52 feet wide and 280 feet long, it lasted until Cheatham Lock and Dam was built, giving the river a nine-foot channel from that dam to Old Hickory Lock and Dam.

**LOCK TWO ROAD** leads north from Pennington Bend Road to the Cumberland River where, on October 9, 1907, Lock Number 2 opened nine miles upstream from Nashville. The cost of construction was $338,618.50. While under construction, it was a favorite spot for the locals to gather on weekends and watch the progress of the lock and dam. They would bring their lunch and spend most of the afternoon relaxing and catching up on the news. By 1914, there was a boat landing where Lock Two Road ended. Lock Number 2 and the dam were demolished by the Army Corps of Engineers when the Cheatham and Old Hickory dams were built.

**LOMBARDY AVENUE** was named by Walter Stokes for the Lombardy District of Italy, the country's most populated and wealthiest region. The street and several others were part of Mr. Stokes's subdivision of Breezemont, his farm on the Hillsboro Pike. In 1935, Mr. Stokes' daughter, Ellen (Mrs. Livingfield) More began construction of her handsome brick home on Lombardy Avenue. Because she wanted a New Orleans flavor, she installed a two-story wrought-iron porch on the back of the house, overlooking a small courtyard. The house was completed in 1936. Lombardy Avenue extends east from Hillsboro Pike to Brightwood Avenue. *See Stokes Lane.*

**LONE OAK ROAD** extends south from Richard Jones Road. Beyond Castleman Drive, it curves east and terminates at Granny White Pike. Lone Oak was named by the John Trotwood Moore family for the giant oak tree that stood at the intersection of Lone Oak and Castleman Drive until it was taken down in 1958. The road was established by the Davidson County Highway Commission in 1919. John Trotwood Moore served as state librarian and archivist from 1919 to 1929.

**LONG HOLLOW PIKE** begins in downtown Goodlettsville at US 31 West and runs northeast into Sumner County. Named because of the long hollow it runs through, the pike passes the site of Mansker's Station, established by Kasper Mansker in 1780 at a salt lick.

**LOUISE AVENUE**, located between Twenty-Second and Twenty-Third Avenues North, was named for Louise Dudley, the daughter of Robert M. Dudley, president of Gray and Dudley Foundry. Louise was killed in the West in 1912. Two years later, my grandfather, Ridley Wills, built a house on Louise

Avenue for his family. It is today's Jimmy Kelly's restaurant. Joel Cheek, the founder of Maxwell House Coffee, lived next door. For a few years, the street was called "Millionaires Row." On June 1, 1925, Mr. and Mrs. Morris Zager were injured when their automobile ran into an old oak tree that stood in the middle of Louise Avenue, just north of its intersection with Elliston Place. The threat of lawsuits against the city for allowing a tree to stand in the middle of a street spelled a controversy that lasted for more than a decade. Sometime after 1935, the tree was taken down. It had been one of only two trees left standing at Burlington after 1864, when Federals used all the fences and all but two trees on the place for firewood.

**LOVE AVENUE** forms the western boundary of the National Cemetery on Gallatin Pike. It was named for the N. O. Love family, whose property was recorded for subdivision in 1914.

**LOVE CIRCLE**, at its top, is known for its spectacular views of the Vanderbilt University campus and downtown Nashville. The street curves up to Love Circle Park at the crest of a 744-foot hill high over West End Avenue, near the Interstate 440 interchange. The hill was the highest point in the old City of Nashville. Love Circle and Orleans Drive were in the heart of Bransford Realty Company's West End Heights subdivision, platted by Ossian B. Simonds & Company, of Chicago, in 1910. Love Circle first appeared in the city directory in 1915. The city built a resevoir under the crest of the hill in 1926 after 8.33 acres were acquired, primarily from John W. Love, after whom the hill was named. Most of the homes on the street were built after 1932.

**LUTON STREET** is in East Nashville. It runs south from Trinity Lane to Gatewood Avenue, parallel to and east of Dickerson Pike. The street was named for I. D. Luton, who developed the property in the 1920s.

**LYNNWOOD BOULEVARD** extends from Harding Pike to the hills beyond Tyne Boulevard and was named for Lynnwood, the Victorian home built by Mr. and Mrs. William Henry Smith on Harding Pike near the intersection of present-day Lynnwood Boulevard and Harding Pike. Lynnwood Park, which included Lynnwood Terrace and the west side of Lynnwood Boulevard from Harding Pike to Westview Avenue, was developed by Pendleton and Blair Realty Company, whose development plat was recorded in 1913.

**MADISON STREET** was named for James Madison, the fourth president of the United States. It is located in North Nashville.

**MAGAZINE STREET** runs north from Division Street, between Eighth and Eleventh Avenues South. It was named for the powder magazine built by the US Army on the site late in the Civil War.

**MAIN STREET**, in East Nashville, becomes Gallatin Pike (US 31 East) at Tenth Street. Neill S. Brown, the only governor of Tennessee to live in East Nashville, resided at an estate on Main Street known as Idlewild. In 1886, the Main Street and Lischey Avenue Street Railroad was chartered to bring electric streetcar service to the area. Hard hit by the fire of March 22, 1916, Main Street lost many buildings, including St. Columbia Catholic Church and the Little Sisters of the Poor home at 521 Main.

**MALONE PLACE**, in Belle Meade, was named for Judge Thomas H. Malone. His home, Honeywood, stood close to the road, adjoining the Belle Meade Deer Park. Judge Malone was first dean of the Vanderbilt Law Department, and a great friend of Judge Howell E. Jackson, who lived at West Meade. Malone and Jackson loved to fox hunt on weekends in the Harpeth Hills. *See Honeywood Drive.*

**MANILA STREET**, between Grenada and Petway Avenues in East Nashville, west of Gallatin Pike, is only one block long. Its claim to fame is that Beth Slater Whitson, who wrote "Meet Me Tonight in Dreamland" (1909) and co-wrote "Let Me Call You Sweetheart" (1910), once lived there.

**MANSFIELD AVENUE** runs east from Neill Avenue to McFerrin Avenue in East Nashville. It carries the name of Mansfield, a home built and occupied by Ephraim H. Foster, United States senator from Tennessee (1843–45). Early in the twentieth century, Mansfield was owned by Capt. John W. Morton, who had been chief of artillery under Gen. Nathan Bedford Forrest.

**MANSKER DRIVE** forms a loop with Cumberland Hills Drive south from Gallatin Pike just before the highway leaves Davidson County and becomes West Main Street in Hendersonville. Mansker Drive was named for Kasper Mansker, the intrepid long hunter who explored this part of Middle Tennessee and built Mansker's Station in 1780, near where Goodlettsville is today.

*Market Street, decorated for the Nashville Centennial Celebration in 1880.*

**MAPLEWOOD LANE** lies between Ellington Parkway and Saunders Avenue in East Nashville. The land on which the lane was built was part of the Maplewood Farm subdivision, the plat for which was recorded in the spring of 1925. The Maplewood house was built by Col. Josiah Williams of Chapel Hill, North Carolina. When the city grew out to the farm, the land became very valuable and its last owner, Col. Jere Baxter, and friends, including J. C. Bradford, chartered the Maplewood Improvement Company to subdivide the property that included lots on Baxter Avenue.

**MARKET STREET** (today's Second Avenue) was first called Main Street. Although there was not a market on the street, it was considered the main thoroughfare to the Market House on the public square. There was also a Market Street in Philadelphia, where early Nashville merchants bought their goods and transported them over the mountains by horseback or in wagons. In the spring of 1866, wooden sidewalks were put down on South Market and both South and North Market were macadamized. In 1888, Market Street was paved with cobblestones from Broad to Church Streets. The street was renamed in December 1904. *See Second Avenue.*

**MAYFAIR ROAD**, between Wilson Boulevard and Lauderdale Road, was subdivided on the plan of Cherokee Park subdivision, the plat for which was filed in April 1928 by the Wakefield-Davis Realty Company of Louisville, Kentucky. Two months later, the same company recorded a plat for the subdivision of Lauderdale Road as far north as Valley Road. This was the second section of the Cherokee Park plan.

**MCCAMPBELL AVENUE** runs northeast from Donelson Pike to Stewarts Ferry Pike. The street was named for the Thomas McCampbell family that lived in the McCampbell-Born House at the corner of McCampbell and Hastings Road. Earlier, Thomas and Elizabeth Bosley Harding lived there with their children. The house, built around 1800, still stands.

**MCCALL STREET** runs east from Nolensville Pike to merge with Antioch Pike. The street was named for J. C. R. McCall, who lived south of McCall Street several hundred feet east of Nolensville Pike.

MCCANN STREET is between Second and Fourth Avenues South, close to City Cemetery. The street was named for Maj. John J. McCann, superintendent of the Model Mill Company.

MCCARN STREET, in East Nashville, was named for Jeff McCarn, a prominent Nashville lawyer who was district attorney in 1908–09. Allison Tidman (Mrs. John) Beasley, is his granddaughter and my friend.

MCCRORY LANE has its northern terminus at US Highway 70. From there it runs south, crossing Interstate 40, beyond which it curves slightly to the east before moving south again to dead-end into State Highway 100, next to the Natchez Trace Parkway exit in the Pasquo community. McCrory Lane was named for one of McCrorys, who were early settlers in Davidson County. Col. Thomas McCrory, a well-known Confederate officer, was the person for whom the McCrory chapter of the United Daughters of the Confederacy was named.

MCFERRIN AVENUE begins at Main Street in East Nashville and runs north to McKennie Avenue. It was named for Rev. John Berry McFerrin (1807–87), Methodist minister and head of the Methodist Episcopal Church South Publishing House. His home stood for many years in what is today McFerrin Park between Lischey Avenue and Meridian Street. The Reverend McFerrin is also remembered for converting and baptizing James K. Polk when the ex-president was on his deathbed in 1849.

MCGAVOCK PIKE was named for the McGavock family of Two Rivers mansion. The portion of the pike near Two Rivers was earlier called Merritt Lane for Judge Alfred Merritt, whose property bounded it. McGavock Pike runs east from Gallatin Pike to the Cumberland River, where, until 1965, a ferry connected it with the longer segment of the road that continues east in Pennington Bend before turning south to end at the Nashville Metropolitan Airport.

Earlier, McGavock Pike, in East Nashville, was Maxey Lane from Gallatin Pike to Oxford Street and Williamson Ferry Road from there to the river. The Williamsons, who had a house in Pennington Bend, operated the ferry that carried horses, cattle, people, bicycles, and, eventually, up to three cars. It was replaced by the seventy-one-ton, eight-car, paddlewheel–driven ferry named for the late county Judge Litton Hickman. The latter ferry was discontinued in 1965, when the Pennington Bend Bridge opened.

The earliest ferry in the bend was the Pennington Ferry that was simply a raft that the ferryman moved across the river by pulling on ropes. It was located a short distance upstream, across the river from Haysborough. The original road on the Donelson side of the river was called Bluff Road because it followed the river bluff.

**MCGAVOCK STREET** begins at Seventh Avenue South and runs west to Ninth Avenue South between Broad Street and Demonbreun. Interrupted by the Frist Center and the railroad gulch, the western section of McGavock picks up at Eleventh Avenue South and extends to Seventeenth Avenue South. The street was named for the McGavocks, possibly the most prominent family in Nashville during the nineteenth century. David McGavock, who moved his family to Nashville in 1794, became the first major landowner in the area. His brother Randall was Nashville's mayor in 1824. Another Randall McGavock, a kinsman of the first, was mayor in 1858. On February 6, 1908, after a heavy snow, more than five hundred people enjoyed riding bobsleds and double-deckers down McGavock Street, coasting from Sixteenth Avenue to Twelfth Avenue.

**MCLEMORE STREET** runs from Demonbreun Street all the way to North Nashville. The portion of McLemore from Church to Cedar (today's Charlotte Pike) was where the stables for all the houses on the west side of Spruce Street (today's Eighth Avenue North) were located. The street was named for John C. McLemore, a clerk in a survey office and a land speculator. He built the first house on the street, near Broad Street. In 2010, the name of the stretch of McLemore Street from Church Street to Charlotte Pike was changed to YMCA Way in honor of the YMCA of Middle Tennessee at 1000 Church Street.

**MCMURRAY DRIVE** connects Edmonson Pike with Nolensville Pike. It was named for Will McMurray, who once owned one of the finest farms in the area.

**MEDIAL AVENUE** was in the heart of a (Walter) Stokes Tract development by Edward Lee Hampton in 1937. Hampton's lots were sold in an area bounded by Golf Club Lane on the south and Compton Road on the northwest.

**MEHARRY BOULEVARD** parallels Jefferson Street from Hadley Park to Twelfth Avenue North. In the 1880s, the street was named Harding Street for

Thomas and Elizabeth Harding, who lived there on land given them in 1837 by her father, Beal Bosley. Thomas Harding was a younger brother of John Harding of the Belle Meade plantation. Sometime after 1910, the street's name was changed to Hefferman Street. In 1931, Meharry Medical College moved there from South Nashville.

In June 1940, the street's name was changed by the city council to Meharry Boulevard in honor of the college that was vitally important in educating African American physicians, dentists, nurses, and other health care professionals. Meharry Medical College was founded in 1876. It was named for Samuel Meharry and his four brothers, Hugh, Alexander, Jesse, and David, who gave more than $30,000 in cash and real estate to the new medical venture of Central Tennessee College. Many large homes on Meharry Boulevard were obliterated during the construction of the interstate through North Nashville in the 1960s.

**MELROSE AVENUE** is between Woodlawn Cemetery and Nolensville Pike. The street was originally named Berry Street for the W. W. Berry family, who lived at Elmwood on Franklin Pike. The name was changed to Melrose for an estate about three and one-half miles south of Nashville near the Franklin Pike that John W. Saunders purchased for his bride, Cynthia, sister of Gideon Pillow. At his death, Saunders willed Melrose to his beautiful widow, who married Aaron V. Brown one month after his inauguration as governor of Tennessee in 1845. Brown died in 1859. During the Civil War, Mrs. Brown, her two daughters, and a son lived alone in the house. Protected by both sides, the house and grounds were "not marred in the slightest degree."[20] Subsequent owners were F. M. Fogg, Edward Sinclair, and William S. Bransford, who bought it in 1912. The house no longer exists.

**MEMPHIS-BRISTOL HIGHWAY** grew out of the Memphis to Bristol Highway Association formed in Memphis in 1911. Soon after the creation of the State Highway Department in 1815, officals in that department named the highway State Route Number 1 and made it their top road priority. Originally, it was a narrow, two-lane road. In the late 1920s, just about the time the highway was completed, the State Highway Department designated the part of the highway from Memphis to Knoxville, through Nashville, as US 70, a national highway that originally ran from Beaufort, North Carolina, to Holbrook,

Arizona. Today, the Memphis-Bristol Highway consists of US 70 and 70 South from Memphis through Nashville to Knoxville, and US 11 West from Knoxville to Bristol. *See US Highway 70.*

**MENZLER ROAD** starts at Murfreesboro Pike one block east of Foster Avenue and runs one-half mile south, paralleling Foster Avenue, to buildings that housed the Tennessee Preparatory School. The school, that closed in 2002, was formerly named Tennessee Industrial School and was at 1200 Foster Avenue. Menzler Street was named for Christian C. Menzler, superintendent of the school in the 1940s and 1950s.

**MERIDIAN STREET** runs north from Foster Avenue to East Trinity Lane, and occupies land purchased by David McGavock in 1786. In 1816, he gave his son, James, the western half of his 640-acre plantation, commonly known as the Fountain Blue tract. James, who had a wife and six children, may have built the two-story brick residence, almost round in shape, that still stands at 908 Meridian Street, shortly before he died. If not, it is likely that his daughter, Lucinda, the wife of Jeremiah George Harris, editor and owner of the *Nashville Union*, built the house later in the 1840s. After retiring from journalism, Harris was appointed disbursing officer in the navy and accompanied Commodore Perry when he opened Japanese commerce to the world in 1854.

In 1865, the Harris' daughter, Lucie Harris Lindsley, inherited the house. Her husband was Dr. Van S. Lindsley. Although they had a house on Spruce Street in town, they probably spent summers at their house on Meridian Street, which was in an area thought to be cooler than the city. At that time, Meridian Street began at Foster Avenue and ended at the Lindsleys' property.

Subsequent owners of the house were Dr. Wesley Gatewood (1891–1905) and educator Alonzo C. Webb, who owned the house from 1905 until his death in 1939. His daughter and executrix, Susannah Webb, sold the house, that had been converted into apartments, two years later. In the ensuing years, the house had numerous owners and tenants.

In 2011, the boarded-up house was owned by the Ray of Hope Community Church of 901 Meridian Street. A church member indicated that the church hoped to renovate the historic house, which has an interesting mural on the second floor, possibly painted by Professor Webb, who also was an artist. The Ray of Hope Community Church formerly was the Meridian Street Methodist

Church, organized in 1925 by combining McFerrin Memorial Church, located at Meridian and Foster, and Alex Erwin Church, located at Douglas Avenue and Dickerson Road.

MIDDLETON PLACE, on the south side of Old Hickory Boulevard between Chickering Road and Hillsboro Pike, was developed by George T. Hicks in the mid 1970s. Its principal street is Middleton Park Lane. George's wife, Sally, named the handsome development for the Middleton Place plantation in Dorchester County, South Carolina, directly across the Ashley River from North Charleston. Started in the eighteenth century and completed in the nineteenth century, Middleton Place was the home of the distinguished Middleton family, including Harry Middleton (1717–84), who served as president of the First Continental Congress, and his son, Arthur Middleton (1742–87), who was a signer of the Declaration of Independence.

MIDDLETON STREET is on Rutledge Hill. It was named for Arthur Middleton, of Charleston, South Carolina, a distinguished Revolutionary War soldier and signer of the Declaration of Independence. He was the father of Septima Sexta Middleton, who married Henry Rutledge, the builder of Rose Hill in Nashville. Rutledge's father was also a signer of the Declaration of Independence.

MOCKINGBIRD ROAD was developed by Wakefield-Davis Realty Company, of Louisville, Kentucky, as part of a Cherokee Park subdivision, the plat for which was recorded on May 14, 1928. The plan encompassed most of the area bounded by Wilson Boulevard, Aberdeen Road, Lauderdale Road, and Harding Pike.

MOLLOY STREET, near the Country Music Hall of Fame, was named for Thomas Molloy, who laid out the original town of Nashville in 1784.

MONROE STREET, in North Nashville, was named for James Monroe, an officer in the Continental Army, minister to France, governor of Virginia, minister to England, secretary of state, and the fifth president of the United States.

MOORMANS ARM ROAD is a connector street linking Whites Creek Pike and Buena Vista Pike in the Bordeaux area. In 1845, Charles W. Moorman purchased about eight acres of land from J. F. Stump "on the waters of White's Creek on the arm of the turnpike leading to the ford of said creek near the place where the road leading from Nashville to Clarksville crosses said creek."[21]

**MORROW ROAD** starts on Charlotte Avenue and runs north and west to end at Sixty-Third Avenue North. It was probably named for the family of Dr. William Morrow, whose home named Westover formerly stood on the state prison farm. The Morrow family lived in Cockrill Bend for over fifteen years.

*This 1865 view looks south toward the State Capitol. It also shows the Church of the Assumption, built in the late 1850s near the intersection of North Vine and Monroe Streets. The house across Vine Street from the church was built by Mr. and Mrs. John H. Buddeke in the late 1830s. It was the first and finest of the mansions built in North Nashville by German-Americn families.*

KERMIT C. STENGEL JR. COLLECTION

**MOSS ROAD**, in Antioch, was originally a dirt road that led from Mt. View Road, behind the former Antioch Baptist Church, east to several farm homes. In the late 1940s or early 1950s, this road was paved and named in honor of magistrate Claude Orville Moss Sr.

**MOSS ROSE DRIVE** is best known as the street on which Roy Acuff, the King of Country Music, lived. From his large colonial home on the river bluff, Acuff enjoyed watching the Opryland theme park being built across the river. (It was later replaced by a mall.) Moss Rose Drive runs from McGavock Pike, on its northern end, to become McGinnis Drive, just north of Shelby Bottoms Park.

**MOUNTAIN VIEW ROAD**, in Antioch, took its name from the Henry Rucker family home called Mountain View that stood on the road until the twenty-first century.

**MURFREESBORO PIKE** (US 41 and US 70 South) has a long history. The Nashville, Murfreesboro, and Shelbyville Turnpike Company was incorporated in 1831. The first high hill it passed leaving Nashville was called Foster's Knob. General Rosecrans used this road to move his Federal Army to Rutherford County in December 1862, prior to the Battle of Stones River. In 1920, when my mother-in-law, Henriette Weaver Jackson, was growing up at Seven Oaks on Murfreesboro Pike, the highway was gravel and had little traffic. Consequently, it was perfectly safe for her and her little brother, William C. "Bill" Weaver Jr., to ride down the road in their pony cart to the Tennessee Hospital for the Insane. Because the Weaver family founded Arlington Methodist Church, Nashvillians sometimes called the Murfreesboro Pike "the Methodist Pike." In the 1930s, the City of Nashville bought 337 acres on the east side of the road, mostly from the related Harris and Weaver families, for the construction of a modern airport. Berry Field opened in 1938, named for Col. Harry Berry, who supervised its construction that was funded by the federal government through the Works Progress Administration. For many years, American and Eastern Airlines had a monopoly on mail, cargo, and passenger service to Middle Tennessee from Berry Field.

*Trevecca Nazarene College, 333 Murfreesboro Pike, was founded in 1901. These are views of Trevecca buildings at five different locations—Fifth and Jo Johnston (1901–1903), 125–29 Fourth Avenue North (1903–1914), Gallatin Road (1914–1932), Whites Creek Pike (1932–34), and Murfreesboro Road (1942–-2011).*

RIDLEY WILLS II COLLECTION

**MURPHY AVENUE** runs from Twenty-Second Avenue North to Twenty-Third Avenue North. It was named for Joseph Murphy, who lived where the Baptist Hospital is today on Church Street.

**MURPHY ROAD** connects West End Avenue with Charlotte Pike. It was also named for Joseph Murphy. Earlier, it was known as West End Boulevard and Minnesota Avenue (1928). The Sylvan Park Restaurant moved to Murphy Road in the early 1940s.

**MUSIC SQUARE EAST** and **MUSIC SQUARE WEST**, east of Broadway, feature many of Nashville's recording studios. Both streets highlight Nashville's reputation as "Music City, USA."

**MYRTLEWOOD DRIVE** goes south from Old Hickory Boulevard near Nipper's Corner. It was named for Mrs. Myrtle Phillips, who owned the land until the 1990s, when it was sold and subdivided into Myrtlewood Estates.

**NALL AVENUE** is in Charlotte Park in West Nashville. It was named for T. M. Nall, who subdivided three lots that formerly belonged to B. W. Cockrill. The subdivision plat was filed on June 6, 1914.

**NASHBORO BOULEVARD** goes east from Murfreesboro Pike to Bell Road near its intersection with Smith Springs Road. The street was named for Fort Nashborough, completed at the Big Salt Lick soon after John Donelson arrived by boat with his party on April 23, 1780. The fort was named for Francis Nash, a Revolutionary War general, who was killed by the British at the Battle of Germantown on October 4, 1777.

**NATCHEZ TRACE** runs south from West End Avenue to Woodlawn Drive. It was originally a part of the Wharton Road, named for Joseph Wharton, who lived west of the present-day intersection of Golf Club Lane and Hillsboro Pike. Later, the road was known as Compton Road, for the prominent Compton families who lived in the hills to the south. Still later, the road was named Twenty-Eighth Avenue South. Most of the homes on Natchez Trace were built in the 1920s and 1930s.

**NATCHEZ TRACE PARKWAY** began during the Depression as a Civilian Conservation Corps project. This two-lane, limited access parkway generally follows the path of the original Natchez Trace. Finally completed on May 21, 2005, the parkway is 444 miles long and connects Natchez, Mississippi, with Nashville. Its northern terminus is at Pasquo, a suburban community in southwestern Davidson County. There, the parkway ends at State Highway 100.

**NATIONAL CEMETERY DRIVE**. *See Riverside Drive.*

**NEBRASKA AVENUE** runs from Fifty-First Avenue North, beside McCabe Golf Course, to Acklen Avenue. The street is in the Sylvan Park neighborhood roughly four miles west of downtown. The name Sylvan Park comes from the Sylvan Park Land Company organized in 1906 by Dr. J. E. Thompson and

James A. Bowling. Bowling's home, Sylvan Park, at 4501 Nebraska Avenue, gave the land company its name. The advent of electric streetcars made the development of Sylvan Park as a residential area feasible. In about 1905, a small streetcar, called a "dinky," ran along Forty-Sixth Avenue, across Nebraska Avenue to Charlotte Pike. It transported Sylvan Park residents to the main streetcar line on Charlotte. From 1927 to 1937, McConnell Field, adjacent to Nebraska Avenue, was Nashville's first municipal airport. It had a large hanger that backed up to greenhouses owned by Geny's Flowers. McCabe Golf Course occupies much of the land that had been McConnell Field.

**NEELYS BEND ROAD** begins at Gallatin Pike and goes east to the bottom of Neely's Bend, opposite the mouth of Stones River on the Donelson side. The bend, lick, and road were named for the William Neely family who lived there. A companion of Kasper Mansker and James Robertson, Neely had been killed and scalped, in 1780, while at camp a short distance from Neely's Lick, where he and companions were making salt. At that time, his daughter, Mary, was kidnapped by the Indians. After escaping several years later, she made her way to Virginia where she married, reared a family, and lived to be ninety years old. In the early 1880s, J. O. Fussell and Thomas Hudson were overseers of two crews assigned to "work" Neelys Bend Road. Jim Pickett, who grew up in Neely's Bend early in the twentieth century, said that he could remember, as a boy, crossing the Cumberland River in a wagon when the water was low.

**NEILL AVENUE**, in East Nashville, was named for Gov. Neill S. Brown, whose home, Idlewild, stood 125 yards north of the intersection of Neill Avenue and Main Street. Brown was governor of Tennessee from 1847 to 1949. In 1850, President Zackery Taylor commissioned Brown as minister to Russia. During his three years in Russia, Mrs. Brown and their children continued to live at Idlewild. By 1909, the Bransford Realty Company had developed one block of Neill Avenue, with homes having been built on all but two of the lots.

**NELSON MERRY STREET** is between George Davis Boulevard and Eighth Avenue North. It honors Nelson G. Merry (1824–84), a free black who became, in 1853, the first ordained African American minister in Nashville. Under Merry, the First Colored Baptist Church became the largest church in the state with two thousand members. During his career, Merry organized at least fourteen Baptist churches.

**NEUHOFF LANE**, near St. Henry's Catholic Church on US Highway 70, was named for Henry Neuhoff. He was the head of the Neuhoff Packing Company, and a prominent member of the church built on land he donated.

**NEWSOM STATION ROAD**, in the extreme southwest part of Davidson County, was named for Joseph M. Newsom, who constructed a turbine-powered gristmill on the Harpeth River in 1862.

**NINETEENTH AVENUE** was formerly named Durham, Douglas, Laura, Rokeby, Everett, and Avondale Streets.

**NINTH AVENUE** was formerly named Vauxhall Place, and Buena Vista, Connor, Deluge, McLemore, and Walker Streets. *See Vauxhall Place.*

**NOELTON LANE** lies one block north of Woodmont Boulevard, and once was on the estate of Mr. and Mrs. Oscar F. Noel. Their home, Noelton, on Granny White Pike, was one of the oldest houses in the area.

**NOLENSVILLE PIKE** (US 31-A and 41-A) leads south from Nashville to Nolensville, a small but rapidly growing Williamson County town on Mill Creek. Originally, the road was named Fishing Ford Road. Nolensville Pike and the community of Nolensville were named for William Nolen, who came to Tennessee from Virginia with his family in 1797. As he was traveling in this area, a wheel on his covered wagon broke in a cane brake, so he stopped to have repairs made. Looking around, he noticed how beautiful the land was and decided to settle there.

In 1868, a group of African American families, many of whom had been slaves, established the Providence community on Nolensville Pike. The name "Providence" came from the fact that they believed divine providence led them to the site.

Cumberland Park, a harness-horse racetrack, was built by Seth Griffin on Nolensville Pike in 1891. The 270-foot-long bandstand that seated seven thousand spectators, and the clubhouse were considered the most elegant and tasteful in the country. In October 1891, Hal Pointer, the Tennessee champion trotting horse, was defeated by Direct, a jet-black stallion from California. Twelve thousand people attended the race.

Cumberland Park became the State Fairgrounds in 1906. Three years later, the Nolensville Pike Swimming Lake, directly on the Nolensville Car Line and adjacent to the State Fairgrounds, opened. The pool, built of concrete, was supplied with clear spring water that flowed from nearby hills. It was surrounded by a beautiful park with benches and electric lights.

For many years early in the twentieth century, gypsies came to Nashville each fall to bury their dead. They camped in a large open field on the Nolensville Pike across from the State Fairgrounds.

The Tennessee Highway Department initially gave numerical names to state highways. A Tennessee highway map, published by the Department of Highways and Public Works in 1934, showed Nolensville Pike as part of State Highway 11 that ran from the Alabama state line through Nashville to the Kentucky state line near Adams, Tennessee.

**NORTH TWELFTH STREET**, in East Nashville, was the site of Edgewood, built in 1854 by Col. Anthony Wayne Johnson, a capitalist, who served in the state senate in 1855 and 1856. In 1872, Johnson gave Edgewood to his daughter, Mary, who was married to John S. Bransford. That same year, their son, Johnson, was born. He would grow up to inherit Edgewood in 1907. Seven years later, Johnson Bransford subdivided the acreage around Edgewood and sold the house at 719 North Twelfth Street. He became one of Nashville's most prominent residential developers, particularly in East Nashville and the rapidly developing West End Area. Edgewood was torn down in 1962.

**NORWOOD DRIVE** was named for the ancestral home of the Kennon family in Virginia. William G. "Bill" Kennon and his wife, the former Elizabeth Thompson, lived on Norwood Drive on land given her by her Thompson family at neighboring Glen Leven. The street, built about 1940, leads directly to Father Ryan High School.

**NURSERY ROAD**. *See Rosebank Avenue.*

**OBSERVATORY DRIVE** is almost U-shaped. It begins at Belmont Boulevard and runs west to curve south and then east, returning to Belmont Boulevard, opposite David Lipscomb University. The street and Burton Avenue were developed as Green Hills subdivision by David Lipscomb College. The plat was recorded on December 16, 1926.

**OLD HARDING PIKE** was named for the Harding family of Belle Meade. The road ran through the middle of Bellevue, which was considered to be the intersection of Old Harding Pike and Bellevue Road. In 1997, there were six different Old Harding Pikes in Bellevue. Because of the confusion this caused policemen, firefighters, and ambulance crews, Bellevue Councilman Vic Lineweaver sponsored legislation that changed the names of four sections of Old Harding Pike to Fred King Road, Sally Morton Circle, Kinnie Drive, and Reasonover View Road, all named for prominent Bellevue residents, all now deceased.

**OLD HICKORY BOULEVARD**, named for President Andrew Jackson, whose nickname was "Old Hickory," completely surrounds Nashville. It is approximately 113 miles in circumference and, as the crow flies, never more than 15 miles from the city. Construction started in 1932 at Cleeses Ferry Road, although the idea of such a road began some years earlier. In July 1936, the highway, still incomplete, was described in the *Tennessean* as "the greatest undertaking, as a single project, in the history of the Davidson County Highway Department."[22] It was then hoped that the entire road would be completed in two years. The section of the boulevard between Granny White Pike and Edmondson Pike was completed in 1936. The road, however, was not fully completed until 2010. Even now, some parts of it are difficult to locate.

**OLD LEBANON DIRT ROAD** still exists in the eastern part of Davidson County. It generally parallels Lebanon Pike but is some distance to the south, running very close to the railroad to Lebanon. When Andrew Jackson went to Nashville by horseback or carriage from the Hermitage, he used this road. The name implies that there is a new Lebanon Dirt Road, but it does not exist. *See Lebanon Pike.*

**OMAN STREET** is a short street behind Centennial Park. For many years in the middle of the twentieth century, Oman Construction Company had its offices here, giving the street its name.

**OMOHUNDRO DRIVE**, between the Cumberland River to the north and Hermitage Avenue to the south, leads to the Omohundro Water Treatment Plant. Both the street and the plant were named for Squire John Omohundro and his wife, Sadie. He was a member of the Davidson County Court from 1924 until his retirement in 1960. Sadie Omohundro was postmaster at Donelson from 1943 to 1954.

**OPRY PLACE**, the site of the Ryman Auditorium, is the short section of Fifth Avenue North between Broadway and Commerce Street. The Union Gospel Tabernacle was constructed in 1882. It was later renamed as the Ryman Auditorium, where Grand Ole Opry performances were held from 1943 until 1973.

**OPRYLAND DRIVE**, in Donelson, leads to the Opryland Hotel and the Grand Ole Opry House from McGavock Pike, just west of its intersection with Briley Parkway.

**ORDWAY PLACE** extends east from Gallatin Pike to North Twentieth Street beside Shelby Park. Ordway Place, Stratton Avenue, and several others were subdivided from the C. F. Ordway home place, following the recording of the plat in June 1888. The 1800 block of Ordway Place is part of "Little Hollywood" because of the 1930s stucco and Spanish-style houses. *See Lakehurst Drive.*

**OTTER CREEK ROAD** begins at Hillsboro Pike and runs east through Radnor Lake State Park to Franklin Pike. The street was named for the Otter Creek, which parallels the road for much of its length.

**OVERTON ROAD** runs south from Hogan Road to Hill Road in Crieve Hall. It crosses land that once belonged to Judge John Overton of Traveller's Rest.

**OVERTON STREET**, in Old Hickory, runs between Eleventh Street and Fifteenth Street and between Sixteenth Street and Robinson Road. The street was named for Gen. Thomas Overton, a Revolutionary War officer and a brother of John Overton, who came to Jones Bend in 1803 with his wife and children and lived there until his death in 1824. He served as Andrew Jackson's second in Jackson's famous duel with Charles Dickinson in 1806.

**OXTON HILL LANE** is located off of Graybar Lane just east of Hillsboro Pike. It was named by developer Dudley Warner II in the late 1990s for the village of Oxton in Scotland. The Warners' friends owned a cottage near the village. *See Channelkirk Lane.*

**PADDOCK LANE** is a short street immediately behind the Belle Meade plantation. It was named for the paddocks that once lined the farm road that eventually became Leake Avenue.

**PAGE ROAD** was named for the Page family. Sallie Harding, a sister of John Harding, married Robert Thomas Page. Their sons, Giles Harding Page and Robert Thomas Page Jr., were members of Capt. Robert Evans's company in the War of 1812. Page Road was initially called Lower Franklin Pike and was used by Elizabeth McGavock (Mrs. William G.) Harding to travel from Belle Meade to her parents' home, Carnton, near Franklin. Today, Page Road extends from Harding Pike to the south, crossing Belle Meade Boulevard at the entrance to Percy Warner Park, and ending at its junction with Chickering Road.

**PARK AVENUE**, in West Nashville, runs west from Forty-Second Avenue North beside Richland Park to Fifty-Third Avenue North. Formerly known as First Avenue, Park Avenue was named for Richland Park. It features a row of attractive Victorian houses facing the park. In the nineteenth century, Philip S. Stump's plantation mansion stood on a slight rise at the southwest corner of today's Forty-Second and Park Avenues. During the Civl War, Stump's home was ravaged by Union soldiers due to his Southern sympathies.

**PARK PLACE** was, in the late nineteenth century, a handsome residential street featuring stately three-story homes, often with their yards enclosed by decorative wrought-iron fences. These houses lined the east side of Park Place that ran between Charlotte Pike and Gay Street immediately east of the Capitol grounds. By the late 1930s, the street was no longer fashionable and the state of Tennessee had acquired seven of the houses. In 1940, the homes were replaced by the Tennessee State Office Building and, in 1952, by the eleven-story Cordell Hull Building. Park Place is now part of Sixth Avenue North.

**PARMER AVENUE,** a short street between Leake Avenue and Scotland Place, was named for Walter O. Parmer, a Nashville horseman, who bought the Belle Meade plantation in 1916 for $55,000. He lived there until his death in 1932. In 1927, a group of Belle Meade citizens petitioned the superintendent of the Davidson County Schools for a grade school in that community. A site was selected on Leake Avenue, and Parmer School, also named for Walter O. Parmer, opened in November 1927. By the following September there were four teachers and grades one through eight. Parmer School closed in 1982 and the building burned down three years later.

**PATTERSON STREET** was formerly named Cumberland Street. It begins at Sixteenth Avenue North and runs west to Twenty-Fifth Avenue North. The street was built shortly after Malcolm Patterson was governor of Tennessee. He served in that capacity from 1907 until 1911. The similarity of names may be coincidental.

*Howell Park, on Peabody Street between Second and Third Avenues North, was named for Morton B. Howell, Nashville's mayor in 1874. The two-acre lot was purchased in 1913 from the University of Nashville (formerly located there). The park was declared surplus in 1967. A condominium occupies the site today.*

KERMIT C. STENGEL JR. COLLECTION

**PEABODY STREET** runs from the river southwest to Seventh Avenue South. It was named for Peabody Normal College, once located two blocks east. Today, the southern terminus of Peabody Street is at Lafayette Street.

**PEACH BLOSSOM SQUARE**, on Craighead Avenue in the West End area, was named for Peach Blossom, the home of Joseph Erwin, whose plantation lay on both sides of the future Richland Turnpike. Erwin's son-in-law, Charles Dickinson, was killed in a duel with Andrew Jackson on May 30, 1806, and was buried on his father-in-law's plantation (today's Carden Avenue).

**PEARL STREET** is between Seventeenth Avenue North and Twentieth Avenue North. It was named for Joshua F. Pearl, Nashville's first superintendent of public schools (1854–61).

**PECAN VALLEY ROAD** goes from Ashland City Road (State Highway 12) and moves northeast, bordering Black Creek, to Old Hickory Boulevard. It was named for a pecan processing plant that was once located on the road.

**PENNINGTON BEND ROAD** leaves McGavock Pike at the busy exit at Opryland Drive. The road runs north, roughly paralleling Music City Drive, before crossing that drive and reversing its course to run south, beside the Cumberland River, to McGavock Pike not far west of its inception. Pennington Bend and Pennington Bend Road were named for John Winfrey Pennington, who was born in 1804. He farmed land in the bend owned by his father, Graves Pennington, and added to the family acreage in the bend. Throughout the 1800s, the bend alternately bore the names Pennington and McSpadden. The first McSpadden to live in the bend was Thomas McSpadden Jr., who bought four hundred acres in the bend in 1809. It is not known when the name officially became Pennington Bend.

**PERCY WARNER BOULEVARD** is between Highways 100 and 70. The boulevard and Percy Warner Park were both named for Percy Warner, a prominent real estate developer.

**PICADILLY ROW** runs west from Una-Antioch Pike before turning south and then east to re-enter Una-Antioch Pike about one-half mile to the south. The street was named for Picadilly Row in London, England.

**PIERCE AVENUE** is a short street that runs from Twenty-First Avenue South to Twenty-Fourth Avenue South immediately north of Vanderbilt's Monroe Carell Jr. Children's Hospital. The short street was named for George Pierce, a bishop in the Methodist Episcopal Church South who vehemently opposed the establishment of Central University (later named Vanderbilt) in Nashville. Pierce particularly objected to the university having a theological school that would have a potential monopoly on Methodist higher education.

**PILCHER AVENUE** is a short street between Thirty-Sixth and Thirty-Seventh Avenues North. It was named for Merritt S. Pilcher. He married into the Barrow family, who owned a mansion in the area.

**POLK AVENUE** runs from Church Street up the hill to Union Street. It is named for James K. Polk, eleventh president of the United States. His home, Polk Place, was situated here, bounded by Church, Spruce, Union, and Vine Streets. Sadly, Polk Place was razed in 1900. It was replaced by a six-story, U-shaped brick apartment building named Polk Flats, built by J. Craig McLanahan.

**PONDER PLACE**, in Metrocenter, was named for Henry Ponder, an important African American educator and president of Fisk University (1984–96).

**PONTOTOC AVENUE**, in East Nashville, was named for the home of John and Willie Evans Fall Early. By 1926, when their youngest child, Elizabeth "Lib," was ten, the Earlys decided to subdivide their property. The plat of the Pontotoc subdivision, that extended from one block south of Early Avenue north to Greenwood Avenue, was recorded on May 19, 1926. By 1933, the Earlys had moved to a new home on Belmont Boulevard. Although Pontotoc was torn down, its handsome stone gates were moved to 3804 Brighton Road, where the Earlys' daughter Kay and her husband, Fred Russell, lived. The Russells' grandson, Russell Harwell, and his family live there today. The gates, with the name "Pontotoc" chiseled in the stone, are still there. *See Early Avenue.*

**POOL AVENUE.** *See P'Pool Avenue.*

**PORTER ROAD** starts at Eastland Avenue and runs northeast and then east to Rosebank Avenue. The road was named for the Porter family who lived for many years at Riverwood mansion. In 1829, Alexander Porter, a wealthy linen merchant, bought a 1795 house and 480 surrounding acres from Dr. Boyd McNairy, who had bought it in 1820 from the builder, Philip Philips. After Porter's death in 1833, his widow, Susan Porter, built a large house close to the original home. She named her new house Tammany Hall. The Porters' grandson, Alexander Porter, renovated the house into a magnificent Greek Revival mansion with six large Corinthian columns across the front. He also combined the old Philips house into the main house. Porter sold the place to Judge William Frierson Cooper in 1859.

Cooper, chief justice on the Tennessee Supreme Court, used the house as a weekend retreat and renamed it Riverwood for the Cumberland River that bordered the property and the surrounding woods. Riverwood is still there at the end of Porter Road.

Next door to Riverwood on Porter Road was Wild Acres, the 508-acre farm of Mr. and Mrs. J. B. Henderson. Mr. Henderson made his wealth as the owner and president of the Southwestern Company. His daughter, Ceacy Henderson Hailey, is a friend of mine. *See Riverwood Drive.*

**POST ROAD** was originally a dirt farm road that ran through H. G. Hill's farm. It was unpaved until after World War II, when H. G. Hill Jr. developed Hillwood Estates. Wentworth Caldwell Jr. recalled, in 2011, of having heard his grandfather, H. G. Hill Sr., say that he named the road for a road in Detroit.[23] Post roads were originally roads used for the conveyance of mail. Post Road connects White Bridge Road with Old Harding Pike, paralleling Richland Creek and Harding Pike to the east.

**POWERS AVENUE** runs north of Eastland Avenue to Tillman Lane. Before the area was subdivided in 1914, the land had belonged to the Robert E. Powers family.

**P'POOL AVENUE** was developed by and named for Dr. David Bruce P'Pool, whose son, Dr. Bruce P'Pool Jr., is a friend of mine. The short street runs north from Elm Hill Pike to become Transit Avenue, just before that street empties into Murfreesboro Pike. During the Depression, Dr. P'Pool bought forty acres of scruffy hillside land consisting primarily of rocks and cedar trees. When AVCO built its plant nearby in 1943, the land gained value. As a result, following the war, Dr. P'Pool built and paved the street, named it for himself, and leased

*The Brass Rail Stables and The Embers were two popular nightclubs in Printer's Alley late in the twentieth century.*

the part of his land facing Murfreesboro Pike to Haynie Gourley, who moved Capitol Chevrolet there. Later, after Mr. Gourley's death, his former partner, Bill Powell, bought the land where the dealership stood. The street is now incorrectly called "Pool Avenue."

**PRENTICE AVENUE**, in Waverly Belmont, runs from Eighth Avenue South to White Avenue. The street was named for Prentice Cooper, governor of Tennessee from 1939 until 1945, and father of Tennessee Congressman Jim Cooper.

**PRINTER'S ALLEY**, originally called Black Horse Alley, was named for the printing and publishing concerns that made it home in the late nineteenth century. At the turn of the century, the Climax Club in Printer's Alley was regionally known as the city's premier entertainment hotspot. During prohibition, Nashville's mayor, Hilary Howse (1909–15 and 1923–38), was asked by a reporter if he would protect Printer's Alley nightspots' illegal selling of whiskey. Howse supposedly said that he would not only *not* close them but would patronize them.

In the late 1950s, Printer's Alley made its mark as a haven for music lovers. Along the alley located between Third and Fourth Avenues North were the Carousel Club, the Club Unique, and the Gaslight. The passage of liquor-by-the-drink in 1967 destroyed much of the excitement of Printer's Alley and the old clubs started to fade away, replaced by seedier establishments.

**PUBLIC SQUARE** was originally laid out in 1784 to include four acres to accommodate future public buildings. The first courthouse was built in 1803. There was, at that time, also a log jail, a pillory, and a whipping post on the square. An 1854 map of Nashville shows a market and a courthouse on the square that was bordered on the west by College Street and on the east by Water Street. Market Street crossed the square between the market and the courthouse. The present Metropolitan Nashville Courthouse dominates Public Square just as it did when it was built in 1937.

**RADNOR STREET** crosses Nolensville Pike and was named for Radnor College, founded by A. N. Eastman in 1906 at the west end of the street. Until the school closed in 1914, President Eastman personally conducted sight-seeing tours by train each summer for young ladies enrolled at Radnor. Fire destroyed the main building in 1921.

*This 1855 view of the public square, looking south and showing a vibriant farmers' market, is thought to be the oldest existing photograph of downtown Nashville. College Street is on the right, to the left is City Hall.*

TENNESSEE STATE MUSEUM COLLECTION

**RAINS AVENUE**, in South Nashville, was named for Capt. John Rains, one of the original settlers of Nashville. Rains built a fort in 1784 that enclosed a spring near today's Rains and Merritt Streets. He owned 640 acres on Brown's Creek and died at age ninety-one.

**RAMSEY STREET**, in East Nashville, runs from South Seventh Street, close to Fred Douglas Park, to Silverdene Place. The street was named for W. B. A. Ramsey, who submitted a plan to subdivide his property in 1855 as "W.B.A. Ramsey's Addition."

*This is the south side of the public square in 1885. The Ensley Building at the far end of the street was on the corner of North First Street and the public square. In 1860, it was considered Nashville's premier commercial building.*

KERMIT C. STENGEL JR. COLLECTION

**REID AVENUE**, near Fort Negley Park, was named for Maj. John Reid, a surveyor and lawyer, who served in the Tennessee General Assembly.

*This 1935 view of the public square shows the Davidson County courthouse, (demolished by February 1936), and the city market, (demolished in 1936–37). The Woodland Street Bridge crosses the Cumberland River as an extention of Deaderick Street.*

**REEVES ROAD**, in Antioch, is named for the Peter Franklin Reeves family that lived in that area for many generations.

**RESERVOIR COURT** is a short street beside and west of Reservoir Park, where the city reservoir stands. The hill was earlier called McCampbell's Hill.

**REVELS DRIVE** crosses Whites Creek Pike north of Moormans Arm Road. The street was named for Hiram Revels, who became the first African American to serve in the US Senate when he represented Mississippi in that body in 1870 and 1871.

**REV. DR. ENOCH JONES BOULEVARD**, in North Nashville, was named for the longtime pastor of the Fifteenth Avenue Baptist Church located at 1203 Ninth Avenue North. The Metro Council approved the name change for a section of Eleventh Avenue North on December 3, 1992.

**RICHARD JONES ROAD,** in Green Hills, south of Hillsboro High School, was named for Richard H. Jones, landscape architect and owner of the Jones Ornamental Nursery that operated at the corner of Hobbs and Estes Roads from 1941 through 1967. Before 1941, Jones operated Howell Nurseries at the same address.

**RICHARDS ROAD,** which runs east-west between Una Antioch Pike and Antioch Pike, was named for George Richards (1815–98), a native of England, who was superintendent of the farm at Central State Hospital. The road was paved in 1953.

**RICHLAND AVENUE,** parallel to West End and one block north of West End, was named for the home of James Robertson in today's West Nashville. Richland Avenue was developed by the Richland Realty Company, organized in 1906. The development company purchased 260 acres and subdivided it into five hundred lots. Three years later, the Bransford Realty Company purchased all the lots on West End and Richland Avenue that the Richland Development Company had left for sale, as well as several hundred feet of frontage on Central Avenue. They put the normal sales restrictions on the Richland Place development. For example, houses facing West End had to cost at least $7,500 and houses on Richland had to cost at least $4,500.

**RICHLAND TURNPIKE** was named for Richland Creek, through which watershed it ran. The turnpike's general route was in existence in 1809, when the road was known as the "Richland Creek and Wharton Road." In 1844, residents in the Harpeth Valley and surrounding area petitioned the General Assembly for a "charter of incorporation for the Richland Turnpike Company" to build a road to the west bank of the Harpeth River, including a bridge over the river.[24] By 1849, three road commissioners reported that the road had been "finished agreeably to the provisions of the charter."[25] The pike began at Boyd Avenue (today's Twentieth Avenue), which was the Nashville corporate line, and led southwest following the present-day West End Avenue and Harding Road through the center of Bellevue. Wilbur F. Foster's 1871 Map of Davidson County identified the turnpike as the "Richland and Harding Turnpike" and indicated that it had a toll gate just before the road ascended today's Nine-Mile Hill. By the end of the nineteenth century, most people called it "Harding Pike," for the Harding family of the Belle Meade plantation.

*This early 1890s view from the top of the main building at Vanderbilt University shows, in the foreground, the university gymnasium, built in 1880, on West End Avenue. The road in the center of the photograph is the Richland Turnpike, that began at Boyd Avenue. Burlington, the W. R. Elliston home, is barely visible facing the turnpike. In the distance is the mile-long West Side Park track that opened in 1887. Beyond it were a half-mile track the grandstand, and a club house.*

Murphy Addition was a large subdivision carved out of the property of Joseph Murphy, a Nashville whiskey tycoon, whose home was on the north side of Richland Turnpike where Baptist Hospital is today. The subdivision extended from Cedar to Church Street and from Boyd Avenue to Centennial Park. It also included a small section, bordered by Boyd Avenue, State Street, Douglas Avenue, and Church Street, called the Boyd Home Track. This subdivision of the Murphy Land Company was recorded in 1904. Two year later, Tom Felder, Murphy's son-in-law, negotiated a contract with Robert T. Creighton, of Foster & Creighton, to grade and macadamize the addition's streets and build sewers, including an extension of the Lick Branch trunk sewer. Over a period of years, fashionable homes were built on Patterson and State Streets in Murphy Addition. *See Harding Road.*

**RIDGEFIELD DRIVE** was built by Tony Sudekum in about 1940 when his company was constructing the Belle Meade Theater. Ridgefield Drive runs between where Sudekum's house, Ridgefield, stood and the theater. The street ends less than one-half mile east, where it connects with Woodlawn Drive.

**RIDGETOP DRIVE**, off of Brick Church Pike, was named for the community of Ridgetop that rides the ridge of the Highland Rim astride the Robertson-Davidson County line. In 1910, the Villa Crest Hotel at Ridgetop was popular with Nashvillians. It was reached by the Louisville & Nashville (L & N) Railroad that had a small passenger station at Ridgetop or by road on what is today's US 41. The hotel advertised itself as "an ideal health and pleasure resort," and bragged about being the highest point between Nashville and St. Louis.[26] In the 1930s and 1940s, there were marvelous house parties at the summer homes owned by wealthy Nashvillians at Ridgetop.

**RIDGEWOOD DRIVE** was subdivided in the late 1950s. It runs along the side of a hill off Chickering Park Drive in Forest Hills. When Charles and Anne Roos bought a lot in 1959, they were pleased with the sheltered location but thought the original name of the street, Sherwood Forest, a bit pretentious. The developer agreed to change the name of the street to Ridgewood Drive, named for the ridge the street climbs.

**RIDLEY BOULEVARD** runs from Bass Street to Edgehill Avenue. The Adventure Science Museum is the most prominent address on the street that was named for C. L. Ridley, a real estate developer with the Waverly Land Company in the late 1880s.

**RIVER ROUGE DRIVE** runs along a limestone bluff on the east side of the Cumberland River near the Rock Harbor Marine Marina. The street was named for River Rouge, Michigan, where the Ford Motor Company had a major assembly plant. The city was named after the Rouge River that flows through it. "Rouge" is the French word for red. *See Comet Drive.*

**RIVER ROAD** (State Highway 251) cuts off Charlotte Pike a short distance beyond where Interstate 40 crosses over Charlotte. River Road generally follows the Cumberland River, for which it was named, to the Cheatham County line. From there, River Road continues to its intersection with State Highway 49 less than one-half mile from the bridge over the Cumberland River to Ashland City. This is a beautiful drive that passes Cumberland Heights Alcohol and Drug Treatment Center.

**RIVERSIDE DRIVE** is shown on various maps as either Riverside Drive or National Cemetery Drive. In 1908, Davidson County agreed to deed to the secretary of war, all that part of Gallatin Turnpike that lay between the Nashville city limits and the National Cemetery, a distance of 4.75 miles. The idea was to widen the narrow road to seventy-five feet and make it a boulevard, providing a fitting approach to the second largest national cemetery in the United States. The County Commission passed a resolution to give the federal government $1,000 annually to keep up the boulevard that the government would pave. National Cemetery Drive never really materialized, possibly because so many Nashvillians were the children of Confederate soldiers, and were not at all interested in building a memorial drive to a Union cemetery.

The first mention of Riverside Drive surfaced in 1911. By November 1912, construction was well underway with three miles of Riverside Drive between the brand new Shelby Park and Gallatin Pike macadamized. This was a county road built by workhouse labor and supervised by its superintendent, George W. Hobson. When finished, the boulevard, a mile or two west of the Cumberland River, would have two twenty-foot driveways with a twenty-foot grass plot in the center and a ten-foot walk on either side.

Because a railroad track separated the southern end of Riverside Drive from Shelby Park, Dr. Rufus E. Fort, whose 350-acre Fortland Farm lay just beyond the park and between it and the river, successfully petitioned the Park Board to build an underpass beneath the railroad track. This would give him and other nearby landowners, including Robert M. Dudley, a more direct access to town. Dr. Fort knew that the City of Nashville had plans to build an extension of Riverside Drive, forty-feet wide, from the Shelby Street through the old Meredith Grove property, over Pugsley's Branch, and through Shelby Park to link up with the section that went by Dr. Fort's farm. Plans for the extension were approved by May 1914.

A 1928 map shows Riverside Drive being complete between Shelby Park and Crutcher Drive near South Seventh Street. The section of Riverside Drive, often called "Double Drive," between Shelby Park and Greenfield Avenue was rededicated in 1933 as a memorial to soldiers in the "Great War." Poppies, the emblem of the war, were planted in the middle greenway. Irises, the state flower, were planted along the border. The memorial was initiated by Louise Fort, Dr. Rufus E. Fort's wife.

A 1939 map of Nashville identified "Double Drive" as Riverside Drive or National Cemetery Road, although the latter road never came to be. The same map does not show Riverside Drive anywhere between Shelby Park and the Shelby Street Bridge. The road identified on the 1928 map as Riverside Drive, between the park and Crutcher Street, was called Davidson Street on the 1939 and subsequent maps.

**RIVERWOOD DRIVE**, in Inglewood, was named for a two-story brick house built in 1833 by Susan Porter, the widow of Alexander Porter, one of Davidson County's most prominent citizens. Mrs. Porter called the original plantation Tammany Hall, and lived there for about twenty years. In 1851, two years before her death, her son, Alexander, enlarged the house, adding six columns across the front and incorporating into the house an older brick house built by Philip Phillips in about 1795, and more recently used by the Porters as a kitchen house.

In 1859, Alexander Porter sold Tammany Hall to William Frierson Cooper, a bachelor and affluent Nashville attorney, who changed the name of the plantation to Riverwood. He used it as a family gathering place. Following Cooper's death in 1909, his half-brother, Duncan B. Cooper, acquired the house.

Duncan's timing was bad as, some months earlier, he and his son, Robin, had a fatal confrontation with Cooper's political enemy, Edward Ward Carmack, on Seventh Avenue North in Nashville. Shots were exchanged, with the result that Robin killed Carmack. The Coopers were found guilty of murder and sentenced to prison, only to have Duncan Cooper pardoned by Gov. Malcolm Patterson. Cooper returned to Riverwood, where he lived until his death in 1922.

His daughter, Sarah Polk Cooper, who had married Lucius E. Burch, inherited Riverwood. Dr. and Mrs. Burch lived there on Porter Road, four miles from Nashville, for many years. Dr. Burch became professor of gynecology and obstetrics at the Vanderbilt Medical School. This expert in clinical work held that position until his retirement in 1945. Riverwood remained in the Porter/Burch family until 1978, when it was sold to Dr. Charles Michael Currie. *See Porter Road.*

**ROBERT E. LEE DRIVE** is between Otter Creek Road and Granny White Pike. The street was developed by Karl Haury and Reese Smith Jr. in the 1960s. It was named for Confederate Gen. Robert E. Lee.

**ROBERTS AVENUE** is a short East Nashville street between Fourteenth Street and Chapel Avenue. In 1915, the Roberts' home stood at the corner of Roberts and Chapel Avenues.

**ROBERTSON ACADEMY ROAD** extends west from Franklin Pike in Oak Hill. The road was named for Robertson Academy, established by an act of the Tennessee General Assembly on September 13, 1806, which provided for an academy in each of the state's twenty-seven counties. The present school, designed by Granbery Jackson Jr., was completed in the fall of 1933. It is currently used by the Metropolitan Nashville Public School System to teach gifted children in a preschool program and for offices for teachers and administrators involved in that program and in early childhood education.

**ROBERTSON AVENUE**, in West Nashville, was named for James Robertson (1742–1814), cofounder of Nashville, whose two-story brick home, originally named Travelers Rest, was built nearby in about 1796. Robertson later graciously changed the name of his home to Richland to avoid confusion with Judge John Overton's home, named Traveller's Rest.

**ROLLAND ROAD** connects Wilson Boulevard, that forms the eastern border of Montgomery Bell Academy, with Bowling Avenue. The road was named for Col. Rolland S. Abrahams by his father, I. K. Abrahams, who owned Abrams Realty Company and who subdivided land nearby.

**ROSA PARKS BOULEVARD** extends from Clarksville Pike next to the Ted Rhodes Golf Course to Broadway. The boulevard was named in 2007 for Rosa L. Parks, who gained fame in a segregated Montgomery, Alabama, when she refused to give up her seat on a city bus to a white passenger. The boulevard was formerly Eighth Avenue North.

**ROSEBANK AVENUE** runs east from Porter Road to its termination just south of Cornelia Fort Airpark. Earlier, the stretch of Rosebank from Riverside Drive east to Preston Drive was called Division. From there to its eastern end, it was called Nursery Road. Rosebank Avenue was named for the many rose bushes that the nursery, started by Ezekial Truett before the Civil War, grew all along the hill beside the avenue.

**ROWAN DRIVE** is in a subdivision off Buena Vista Pike in which many of the streets were named for prominent African Americans. Rowan Drive was named for Carl T. Rowan (1925–2000), who grew up in McMinnville, Tennessee, and who attended Tennessee A & I University. Rowan was a nationally syndicated columnist for the *Washington Post* and the *Chicago Sun-Times*. He was one of the most respected African American journalists of the twentieth century.

**ROY ACUFF PLACE** extends from Eighteenth Avenue South across Music Square West to Music Square East. The street was named for Roy Acuff, whose well-deserved nickname was the "King of Country Music." He became a member of the Grand Ole Opry in 1938 and, in 1962, was the first living member to be elected to the Country Music Hall of Fame.

**ROYAL OAKS PLACE** is a short street that extends one block north of Iroquois in Belle Meade. It was named for Royal Oaks, the home of Mr. and Mrs. W. J. Cummins on Harding Pike. Cummins Station, on Tenth Avenue South, was also named for W. J. Cummins, a successful Nashville businessman who moved to New York City.

**RUSSELL STREET** is one of the principal residential streets in East Nashville. It runs from First Street to Shelby Park, and features many handsome homes from the late nineteenth and early twentieth centuries. The street was named for Russell Houston, a real estate speculator, who, with Felix Zollicoffer and others, subdivided the land between Fatherland and Shelby Streets and Second and Fifth Streets into fifty lots before the Civil War. The East Nashville fire of March 22, 1916, destroyed virtually all the homes on Russell between Sixth and Seventh Streets.

**RUTLEDGE STREET** runs south from Peabody Street to Lea Avenue in South Nashville. Both Rutledge Street and Rutledge Hill were named for Edward Rutledge, signer of the Declaration of Independence. He was the father of Henry Middleton Rutledge, who lived on the hill, with his wife, Septima Sexta Middleton Rutledge.

**RYMAN ALLEY** was named for the Ryman Auditorium on its north side. The alley runs from Opry Place to Fourth Avenue North. It is famous because the

*This charming street scene from about 1900 looks northeast to the Edgefield Baptist Church at 700 Russell Street. The little girl is riding a new "safety" bicycle, complete with wheels of the same size and pneumatic tires.*

MARTHA ANN BARRICK CALDWELL COLLECTION

back door of the Ryman Auditorium connects with Tootsie's Orchid Lounge directly across the alley. During the years 1943–1973, when the Grand Ole Opry was held in the Ryman Auditorium every Saturday night, entertainers like Hank

Williams could step out of the Ryman through the back door and enter Tootsie's for a beer before returning for their next performance. Better yet, they could do so without anyone on Fifth Avenue seeing them.

ST. JAMES PLACE was developed by Vernon Sharp in the 1960s as part of a Chickering Lane extension of Chickering Road. Initially, Mr. Sharp intended to name the street Chevy Chase, but William B. "Bill" Akers, who bought property on the street, didn't like the name and asked Mr. Sharp to consider changing it. Mr. Sharp complied and renamed the street St. James Place and a neighboring street Piccadilly Place.

SAVANNAH PLACE is a short street off of Lealand Lane in the Glendale area. It took developer Dudley Warner II fourteen years of negotiation and successful litigation in chancery court to complete the development in the late 1990s. He named the street for Savannah, Georgia.

SAWYER BROWN ROAD's northern terminus is at Old Charlotte Pike. From there, the road runs south to Old Harding Pike. Sawyer Brown Road goes by the site of a two-story frame house built in 1834 by Aris Brown. The Sawyer farm was nearby. There were three Sawyer brothers: Dempsey (considered the patriarch), Coston, and J. R.

SCOTLAND PLACE is a block-long street behind the Belle Meade plantation. It was named for Bonnie Scotland, the great stallion whose paddock was located there.

SECOND AVENUE was formerly named Market Street. Today, it runs from just north of Cement Plant Road in North Nashville to Lafayette Street in South Nashville. The Nashville Race Course, also called the Burns Island Track, was located, from 1828 until 1884, near what is now Second Avenue North and Van Buren Street. The racetrack was the scene of the $25,000 Peyton Stakes on October 16, 1843, at the time the richest race ever run. The winner, Peytona, was owned by Nashvillian Thomas Kirkman. *See Market Street.*

SEDBERRY ROAD begins at Davidson Road and runs south, crossing Cargile Road before curving into Post Road. One story is that Sedberry Road was named for the Sedberry Hotel in McMinnville, known for its excellent food. The more likely version is that the street was named for Eleanor (Mrs. Neil) Cargile's family. Her maiden name was Eleanor Sedberry Allen. *See Cargile Lane* and *Cargile Road.*

**SEVENTEENTH AVENUE** was formerly known as Salem (north of Buchanan), James, Addison, West Belmont, and South Boulevard Streets. The mayor and the city council gave final approval to the name change in December 1904. In the mid- to late-nineteenth century, Alex and Louise Warner lived on today's Seventeenth Avenue North near Fisk University. The Warner family was one of the prominent German-American families in Nashville.

**SEVENTH AVENUE** was formerly named Vine Street. Its northern end is in North Nashville at Coffee Street, while the other end is at Division Street in South Nashville. The State Capitol grounds cause an interruption in the street between the State Library and Archives and James Robertson Parkway. *See Vine Street.*

**SEVIER STREET** runs, in broken segments, from South Tenth Street to Shelby Park. It was named for John Sevier, an intrepid Indian fighter who, in 1796, became the first elected governor of Tennessee. After three terms as governor, he was elected to Congress. In 1889, Boscobel College for Young Ladies opened in the former Shelby Williams mansion on an elevated ten-acre wooded site on Sevier Street that overlooked the Cumberland River. The purpose of the school, that focused on art and music, was to provide higher education at the lowest possible cost to young ladies. At its peak in the 1890s, Boscobel College had over one hundred students. The college closed in 1914. The building remained until 1940, when it and thirty-nine other structures were cleared to build public housing that would be named for James Cayce, chairman of the Nashville Housing Authority Board, who died while the project was being completed.

**SEWANEE ROAD**, in Oak Hill, begins at Granny White Pike and runs east before turning sharply south to dead-end into Overton Lea Road. Sewanee Road was named for Sewanee (The University of the South), where Luke and Overton Lea went to college. Luke and Overton grew up at Lealand, their parents' country home, that was reached from Granny White Pike by a mile-long driveway. Sewanee Road was built on Lealand lands.

Governor's Mansion,
7th Ave., Nashville, Tenn.

*This circa 1914 view is of the 300 block of Seventh Avenue North, looking from Union Street toward Cedar Street. The tower of the State Capitol rises above the handsome homes on the east side of the street. The house on the immediate right, at 314 Seventh Avenue North, was the state's first executive residence. Five governors lived there between 1907 and 1921.*

RIDLEY WILLS II COLLECTION

**SHARONDALE DRIVE** was originally spelled "Sharendale." It first appeared in the 1912 city directory. The street runs from Woodlawn Drive to Hillsboro Pike. For many summers, through 2010, a popular flower market operated out of a tent on Sharondale in the front yard of Trinity Presbyterian Church.

**SHARPE AVENUE** crosses Gallatin Pike and extends east to Chapel Avenue. It may have been named for W. A. Sharp, who developed a revised plan of A. M. Hooker's Addition between Seymour and Petway Avenues in 1918.

**SHAWNEE DRIVE**, near the intersection of Davidson Road and Charlotte Avenue, was named for the Shawnee tribe living in the Cumberland Country from about 1665 until 1714, when many of them were massacred by Chickasaws above the mouth of the Harpeth River. Those who survived migrated north to the Green River in the future state of Kentucky, and to the Wabash, in what would become Indiana. The Shawnee's most famous chief was Tecumseh, who sided with the British in the War of 1812, and who was killed in the Battle of the Thames in 1813.

**SHAWNEE ROAD**, in Neelys Bend, was also named for the Shawnee Indians.

**SHELBY AVENUE** was named for Dr. John Shelby, a prominent Nashville physician, who lived in the area that later became Edgefield, until that town was incorporated into Nashville in 1880. At Ninth Street, Shelby Avenue climbs Confederate Hill. In 1873, Bishop Holland McTyeire, having secured a pledge of $500,000 from Commodore Cornelius Vanderbilt to fund a university in Nashville bearing his name, began scouting out possible sites for the school. McTyeire, who had lived in Edgefield from 1854 until 1862, was urged by his former neighbors to put the school in East Nashville. Consequently, he considered Confederate Hill before choosing Litton Hill west of Nashville between West End Avenue and Hillsboro Pike. In 1910, neighborhood families gathered on Confederate Hill to watch Hailey's Comet. Despite losing out on Vanderbilt, Confederate Hill did have a college. Boscobel College was on its lower slopes to the south from 1889 until 1914.

After traversing Confederate Hill, Shelby Avenue continues on eastward to Shelby Park, which was dedicated on July 4, 1912, by Mayor Hilary Howse and the Park Board. The mayor called Shelby Park "the most beautiful natural park in the Southland."[27]

The Shelby Avenue Bridge (also called the Sparkman Street Bridge), completed in 1909, was constructed as a way for city reformers to get rid of a slum area on the west side of the bridge called "Black Bottom." The bridge, designed by Howard M. Jones, chief office engineer for the N. C. & St. L. Railroad, and built by Foster & Creighton Company, served as a vital link between East Nashville and downtown.

Shelby Bottom, also named for Dr. John Shelby, encompassed the area between Shelby Avenue and the river. Willow trees and scrub growth dominated the bottom along with a large pond, stagnant in summer. The algae on the surface and the mud bottom made the pond unsuitable for swimming. In the winter, however, the pond was a favorite spot to ice skate.

**SHELTON AVENUE** proceeds east from Gallatin Pike to its termination at Golf Street. In 1933, the Inglewood Country Club moved to the corner of Stratford and Shelton Avenues. In the mid-1930s, the Inglewood Golf Club Addition was built. Shelton Avenue was named for P. A. Shelton, an investor in the Inglewood Land Company. Dr. Cleo Miller, founder of Miller's Clinic on the Gallatin Pike, built his home, Ivy Hall, designed by Edwin Keeble, on Shelton Avenue in 1936. The Millers and their four children (Jack, Jimmy, Bernice, and Jean Ann) also had the first privately-owned clay tennis court in town.

**SHEPARD PLACE**, in Belle Meade, was opened in 1916. Initially, it extended from Jackson Boulevard east one block to the Belle Meade stonewall. Five years later, Shepard Place was extended down the hill to Belle Meade Boulevard. The street was named for David Alexander Shepherd (1879–1959) of Sewanee. He was a partner in the Belle Meade Park Company, organized in 1913, and a life-long friend of Luke Lea, who developed the street. Shepherd, who graduated from Sewanee in 1900, a year behind Luke Lea, went on to teach at Baylor School and Sewanee Military Academy, and to become national chairman of the Sewanee Alumni Association from 1920 to 1923.

**SHUTE LANE** was named for the Shute family, of German descent, who came to Davidson County in 1790. The lane begins at Old Hickory Boulevard and runs east and south to terminate at Lebanon Pike. In 1921, the state of Tennessee acquired one hundred acres of pasture land on Shute Lane, adjacent to the Hermitage, to be used primarily by the 105th Observation Squadron of the Tennessee National Guard. The field was named for H. O. Blackwood, who contributed $1,000 of the $4,000 needed to purchase the land. On July 29, 1924, the first airmail flight from Nashville took off from Blackwood Field. With increased airplane activity, the members of the Ladies Hermitage Association became increasingly fearful that one of the "flying machines" would fall on the Hermitage. Their pressure and the need for a more centralized airport caused Blackwood Field to close in 1928. Its replacement, McConnell Field in West Nashville, opened in 1927.

**SHY'S HILL ROAD** crosses Harding Place between Hillsboro Pike and Granny White Pike. The street was named for Col. William H. Shy, CSA, who was killed while defending the hill during the Battle of Nashville on December 16, 1864.

**SIDCO DRIVE** is an abbreviation of Suburban Industrial Development Corporation and runs due south from Thompson Lane between the CSX railroad tracks to the east and Powell Drive to the west. Nashville businessmen Dewitt Carter, Don Creighton, Bob Crichton, and John McDougal bought the property at auction after the Classification Center closed in 1944. The men systimatically sold off property in the industrial park to such companies as H. G. Hill. *See Thompson Lane.*

**SILLS DRIVE** is a short street off of Lambert drive in Oak Hill, between Franklin Pike and Interstate 65. The street was named for Floyd Sills, treasurer of Foster & Creighton Construction Company.

*Great War veterans from the Thirtieth Division parade down Sixth Avenue North in September 1936. The man in the white suit holding the 117 Infantry sign is passing in front of the Andrew Jackson Hotel. The end of the parade is crossing Union Street in front of the Hermitage Hotel.*

NASHVILLE BANNER, SEPTEMBER 29, 1936, JAMES G. STAHLMAN COLLECTION, NASHVILLE ROOM, NASHVILLE PUBLIC LIBRARY

SIXTEENTH AVENUE was, until its name changed in December 1904, known as North Webster, Hendershott, Odd, Park, Belmont, and East Belmont Streets.

SIXTH AVENUE was formerly named Darmstadt, Park Place, and High Streets. In the 1950s, some of the best men's stores in Nashville were on Sixth Avenue North between Church and Union Streets. They included Levy's Inc., Mallernee's Inc., and Jarman Shoes. B. H. Stief Jewelry Company, the city's finest jewelry store, and Nashville Trunk & Bag were in the same block. *See High Street.*

SMITH SPRINGS ROAD begins at Murfreesboro Pike near the Nashville International Airport. The road runs east through the Smith Springs community to terminate at Percy Priest Lake near Smith Springs Park. Early in the twentieth century, several men in the Smith Springs community began worshiping each Lord's Day in an old lodge adjacent to the school on Old Anderson Road near Smith's Spring. On November 21, 1907, Ms. Nancy Moore deeded an acre of land, located at the corner of Smith Springs Road and Old Anderson Road, to Tom M. Hill, John Lane, and C. W. Brewer. The land included the spring, which supplied water during the dry summer months to people for miles around. They built a one-room frame church building on this land. The community, the Smith Springs Church of Christ, and Smith Springs Road were all named for the spring. Earlier the road was called Dry Branch Road.

SOCIETY ALLEY runs parallel to Woodland Street midway between it and Russell Street, from Eighth Street to Ninth Street. It was named because of the members of high society who lived on Russell and Woodland Streets during the late nineteenth and early twentieth centuries. The conductors of the streetcar line would often cry out, "Eighth Street, Ninth Street, Society Alley." Late on Friday and Saturday evenings, some streetcar passengers would be dressed in evening clothes.

SOUTH DOUGLAS AVENUE stretches from Twelfth Avenue South to Eighth Avenue South at Douglas Corner. There, until 1957, stood Belle Vue, the home of Mrs. Bruce Douglas. The fourteen-room brick house was built in 1840 by Robert Woods, and was in the middle of his large farm on Franklin Pike. W. T.

Berry bought the house in 1848 that, in time, was passed down to his grand-daughter, Mrs. Douglas. Berry's father-in-law, Wilkins Tannehill, a historian and publisher, lived in the house late in his life. Douglas Avenue was built in the late 1880s as part of the Waverly Land Company subdivision, for which Douglas Avenue formed the southern border.

**SOUTH SIXTH STREET** begins at Main Street and runs south to Davidson Street beside the Cumberland River. In the 1890s, Pugley's Gut, at the foot of South Sixth Street, was a favorite place for East Nashville boys to swim.

**SPENCE LANE** connects Murfreesboro Pike and Cave Road near Demonbreun's cave. The Nashville Railway and Light Company operated a small electric streetcar called a "dinky" on Fairfield Street to Spence Lane.

*South Sixth Street, showing the devastation of the East Nashville fire of March 22, 1916, that destroyed 648 homes and left three thousand people homeless.*

TENNESSEE STATE LIBRARY AND ARCHIVES

**SPRING STREET** began at Water Street and ran west. It was named for the bold spring located between College and Market Streets near the foot of Spring Street. The spring flowed east to the Cumberland River at the bluff. It is said that this spring was within the fort built by members of the Robertson party in 1780. In the spring of 1866, the street was macadamized. That same year, its name was changed to Church Street because Christ Episcopal, McKendree Methodist, and First Presbyterian Churches had sanctuaries on the street. *See Church Street.*

**SPRING VALLEY ROAD** was named for the ever-flowing spring near the street just south of Lebanon Pike in Donelson.

**SPRUCE STREET** (now Eighth Avenue) was named after the spruce tree. In the 1880s, Spruce Street, between Church Street and Broad, was described in this charming way: The street was "shaded by huge spruce and maple trees, the mansions along both sides separated one from the other by prim iron picket fences, the gardens in back enclosed by high brick walls. Down this street and the adjoining avenues, the gentry of that period were wont to go, in victories and coaches, in quest of their separate and sedate pleasures."[28] *See Eighth Avenue.*

**STANFORD DRIVE** was developed by Stanford and Criswell Developers. The subdivision contained fifty-five lots along the drive that makes a loop on the east side of Hillsboro Pike. During the late 1930s, numerous homes were built along this street named for R. D. "Bob" Stanford, one of the developers. In 1938, Neely Coble and his wife, Mary, bought four acres on South Stanford Drive, where they built their house. Their total expenditure was $12,000.

**STATE HIGHWAY 100** is a continuation of Harding Pike. Just beyond Page Road, US Highway 70 veers slightly to the right and crosses a bridge over the railroad. State Highway 100, which was completed on November 1, 1928, continues straight ahead. Before Interstate 40 was built, motorists traveling between Nashville and Memphis could either go on US 70 through Dickson, Waverly, and Huntingdon, or on State Highway 100 through Centerville, Linden, Henderson, and Whiteville, where Highway 100 ends. To continue west to Memphis, travelers would pick up US 64. During the 1930s and 1940s,

Nashvillians drove out Highway 100 to swim at the privately-owned Clearwater Beach on the South Harpeth River near Pasquo.

**STEWART'S FERRY PIKE** was divided into two pieces following the creation of Percy Priest Lake, completed by the US Army Corps of Engineers in 1967. The western portion runs from Lebanon Pike southeast to the lake. The eastern section continues east. The pike was named for Stewart's Ferry on Stones River, built in the early 1800s by Andrew Stewart. He was possibly a son of William Stewart, who was killed by Indians in 1792. In 1787, William Stewart lived near Judge John Haywood's home, Tusculum. He also owned a preemption of 640 acres lying on the east side of Stones River south of Stoner's Lick.

*This is an aerial view of the Tennessee School for the Blind at 115 Stewarts Ferry Pike, taken soon after it opened in 1952. Operated by the Tennessee Department of Education, the school serves visually impaired day and residential students from kindergarten through high school. Lebanon Pike (US Highway 70) is visible at the bottom of the picture.*

RIDLEY WILLS II COLLECTION

**STIRRUP DRIVE**, in Bellevue north of US 70, is part of a themed subdivision that has other horse-related names such as Bridle, Harness, Saddle, and Carriage Drives.

**STOKES LANE** runs from Hillsboro Pike east to Belmont Boulevard. It was named by Walter Stokes, whose home, Breezemont, stood on a hill three miles south of town on the Hillsboro Pike. Mr. Stokes built Stokes Lane (one-half mile south of where Breezemont stood) and Lombardy Avenue at the same time. Both show on a 1939 map of the city. *See Lombardy Avenue.*

**STONEWALL DRIVE** parallels Kirkman Lane to the north. It goes from Sewanee Road to Lealand Lane, and was named for the stone walls beside the road that served Confederate Gen. A. P. Stewart's corps so well on December 16, 1864, the second day of the Battle of Nashville.

**STONEWALL STREET** was today's Fifteenth Avenue between Cedar and Church Streets. It was named for a stone wall that ran along the front of the state penitentiary located there from 1832 until 1897, when the penitentiary moved to a 3,500-acre site in Cockrill Bend. *See Fifteenth Avenue.*

**SUMMER STREET**, one of Nashville's oldest streets, was home to two of the city's oldest churches, St. Mary's Catholic Church and the First Presbyterian Church. The street was probably named for the season of the year. Wooden sidewalks were put down on Summer Street in the spring of 1866, and a bridge was built across Wilson Spring Branch south of Broad. Summer Street became Fifth Avenue, North and South, in December 1904. *See Fifth Avenue.*

**SWEETBRIAR AVENUE** goes from Hillsboro to Belmont Boulevard. The oldest house on the street is at 2000 Sweetbriar. It is a Victorian, one-story house featuring dark brick, a hipped roof, and a polygonal bay on the right, balancing the porch on the left. Sweetbrier Avenue was, in 1909, part of Belmont Heights, a development of Belmont Land Company managed by Paul Davis. Belmont Heights featured sidewalks, macadamized streets, fine drainage, easy access to the Belmont Heights car line, and views of the Brentwood hills to the south.

*This 1885 photograph was taken at the intersection of Summer and Church Streets. The building on the corner was leased in 1904 by the then-named Cain & Sloan Company, who occupied it and the building next door until 1957, when Cain-Sloan Company moved to its new building across Church Street. The next building on Summer is the Thompson Brothers elegant Dry Goods Store at 14 North Summer Street. Notice the gas arch light over the Street.*

KERMIT C. STENGEL JR. COLLECTION

**TANGLEWOOD DRIVE** parallels Brush Hill Road near the original Haysborough settlement on the north bank of the Cumberland River. The street was named by Robert M. Condra, a prominent Nashville builder, who developed the Tanglewood Historic District from the 1920s to 1940s. Cabins at Tanglewood feature logs, some of which are thought to have been taken from original Haysborough cabins. Several politicians, including Hillary Howse, mayor of Nashville from 1923 until his death in 1938, had summer cottages there. Charlie Daniels recorded several songs at the largest cabin because of its wonderful acoustics.

**TANKSLEY AVENUE** runs east from Nolensville Pike, two blocks south of Thompson Lane, to Dobbs Avenue. This Glencliff area street was named for the developer, W. T. Tanksley. The subdivision was developed in the 1920s.

**TENTH AVENUE** was, until 1904, named Crooked, Maple, North, Polk, Belleville, Walnut, Gowdy, Malvina, Fairmount, Harris, Dixon, Longview, Gardener, and Currey Streets, and Jowett Avenue.

**TERRACE PLACE** runs from Twentieth Avenue South to Twenty-First Avenue South, one block east of West End Avenue. When my grandparents, Dr. and Mrs. Matt B. Gardner, moved to 2000 Terrace Place in 1893, the street was lined with stately homes and brick sidewalks. In the early 1900s, four Vanderbilt fraternities (Sigma Nu, Kappa Alpha, Beta Theta Pi, and Phi Kappa Psi) owned houses at 2007, 2009, 2013, and 2016 Terrace Place, respectively. By the middle of the twentieth century, Terrace Place was still a residential street.

**THIRD AVENUE** was formerly named College Street because it led directly from the town to the University of Nashville on Rutledge Hill in South Nashville. Today, Third Avenue North goes from downtown to Interstate 65, where it becomes Dominican Drive. Third Avenue South stops at Houston Street. *See College Street.*

**THIRTEENTH AVENUE** was named Morgan Street before December 1904.

**THIRTIETH AVENUE** was, before December 1904, Amelia and Williams Streets.

THOMPSON LANE is a major urban thoroughfare that runs from Franklin Pike to Murfreesboro Pike. It passes through lands once owned by Thomas Thompson, who traveled overland with James Robertson to the Cumberland Bluff in 1779. Originally, Thompson Lane ran from Franklin Pike to Nolensville Pike. In 1877, Joseph Hamilton Thompson, a grandson of Thomas Thompson, built his home, Brightwood, in the middle of a beautiful grove of trees where the Pepsi Cola Bottling Company plant stands at 715 Thompson Lane.

In 1942, the US Army Air Force leased a large tract of land along the south side of Thompson Lane between Franklin Pike and the railroad and built a Classification Center where cadets were brought for preliminary training,

*This view of Thompson Lane, looking west, was taken about 1910 from the front gate of Brightwood, the home built by Joseph Hamilton Thompson in 1877. The house was situated in a beautiful grove of trees on a rise above the eastern branch of Brown's Creek. Today, the Pepsi Cola Bottling Company occupies the site.*

MRS. JAMES E. CALDWELL, COMPILER,
*BEAUTIFUL AND HISTORICAL HOMES IN AND NEAR NASHVILLE, TENNESSEE*

aptitude tests, and physical examinations before being shipped to other bases for further training. The center eventually encompassed 560 acres before it closed in 1944. At its height, the Classification Center had a staff of two hundred officers, five hundred enlisted personnel, and housed an average of ten thousand soldiers per year. After the war, the temporary buildings were torn down and the site became Nashville's first planned and controlled industrial development area, known by its acronym, SIDCO. *See Sidco Drive.*

**TORBITT STREET**, one block south of Clifton Avenue in North Nashville, was named for Granville C. Torbitt, who married into the prominent Barrow family.

**TRINITY LANE**, a major east-west corridor in East Nashville, was originally called Countess Street. The petition to build the road from Dickerson Pike to Gallatin Pike was presented to the commissioners of the Davidson County Quarterly Court in September 1844.

**TRUXTON DRIVE**, off Stewarts Ferry Pike in Donelson, is not far from the site of the Clover Bottom Racetrack, where Truxton, one of Andrew Jackson's best racehorses, once raced.

**TULIP GROVE ROAD** runs south from Lebanon Pike to Central Pike. It was named for historic Tulip Grove, the home of Andrew Jackson Donelson, and his wife, Emily.

**TUSCULUM ROAD** crosses Interstate 24 north of Old Hickory Boulevard. It is named for Tusculum, the home of John Haywood, who named his home for Cicero's home outside Rome.

**TWELFTH AVENUE** was formerly named Songster, Florence, and McNairy Streets, and, after passing Stevens Street, the remaining part of Kayne Avenue.

**TWENTIETH AVENUE** was formerly known as Crook, Boyd, Corinne (named for Corinne Hayes Lawrence, sister of Adelicia Hayes), and Courtney Streets.

**TWENTY-EIGHTH AVENUE** was formerly Beck, Euclid, Clare, Barrow, Archibald, Palmer, and West Horton Streets.

*This 1974 photograph shows, from left to right, four buildings on the Peabody campus: North Hall, the Cohen Art Building, the Administration Building, and the library. On the north side of Twenty-First Avenue South, the two most prominent buildings are the eleven-story Oxford House on the left, and the Medical Arts Building on the right. Beyond the parking lots is the Veterans Administration Hospital.*

SCHMIDT, GARDEN & ERIKSON, CHICAGO

**TWENTY-FIFTH AVENUE** was, before December 1904, Lane, West Robertson, Plunket, Maddin, and Brown Streets. Norman Farrell, mayor of Centennial City in 1897, lived on today's Twenty-Fifth Avenue. Centennial City was incorporated in 1897 to control the environment in and around the Tennessee Centennial Exposition that was outside the Nashville city limits. Farrell is credited with having first proposed the idea of changing the names of the first thirty north-south streets west of the river to numbered avenues. In 1895, when he subdivided his property, he called the new street Twenty-Fifth Avenue because he counted off the streets from the river to his subdivision and found that the river was twenty-five blocks away.

**TWENTY-FIRST AVENUE** was formerly Estrella and Tweed Streets, and Vanderbilt Avenue, from West End Avenue to Garland Avenue. Vanderbilt

Avenue formed the northern and eastern borders of the Vanderbilt campus. When I was a Vanderbilt student in the 1950s, I spent a considerable amount of time at Ireland's, a restaurant at 204 Twenty-First Avenue South that catered to Vanderbilt students, and was famous for its steak and biscuits.

**TWENTY-FOURTH AVENUE** was formerly Commons, Abbott, McEwen, Farrell, and Carlyle Streets.

**TWENTY-NINTH AVENUE** was formerly named Jockey and Vernon Streets.

**TWENTY-SECOND AVENUE** was formerly Alamo and Felder Streets.

**TWENTY-SEVENTH AVENUE** was formerly Butler Street.

**TWENTY-SIXTH AVENUE** was formerly named Unknown Street.

**TWENTY-THIRD AVENUE** was formerly Laland and Elliston Avenues and West Street.

**TWO RIVERS PIKE** connects Briley Parkway and McGavock Pike near the historic Two Rivers home, named by its first owner, William Harding, for the adjoining Cumberland and Stones Rivers. Today, the city owns the historic Two Rivers mansion.

**TYNE BOULEVARD** extends from Hillsboro Pike east to the Franklin Pike. It was named for Thomas J. Tyne, one of the founders of the National Life and Accident Insurance Company in 1901. Tyne family members have lived at Longleat, on the corner of Tyne and Hillsboro Pike, since the house was purchased and remodeled by Mr. and Mrs. Tyne in 1930.

**UNA ANTIOCH PIKE**, in Antioch, was paved in the early 1930s and is an extension of Antioch Pike. It and the Una community are named for Una Jones, a beautiful Texan who once boarded with the Harwood family in the area while attending Peabody College.

**UNION HILL ROAD** begins at Whites Creek Pike in Joelton. It runs northeast and ends at Greer Road at Union Hill. James Galbreath (1871–1967) believed that the name Union Hill Road came from the fact that, in a distance of one mile, the road that crossed the hill united seven roads. He called this a "union of roads."

**UNION STREET** was originally called Union Alley. It still runs east-west in downtown Nashville between Church Street and Charlotte Avenue. A considerable portion of Union Street was macadamized and graveled in the spring of 1866. In July 1896, the city council appropriated $6,000 to widen Union Street. It still is one of downtown's narrowest streets. In the 1940s–60s, Loveman's, on the corner of Fifth and Union, was one of Nashville's leading department stores, competing with Cain-Sloan and Harvey's.

*This 1880s view of Union Street looks east from Summer Street. The five-story Cole Building was on the corner of Union and Cherry Streets. It was built in 1882 by Edmund W. Cole.*
RIDLEY WILLS II COLLECTION

UNIVERSITY STREET still exists in abbreviated form. In 1898, it ran from Lafayette Street to Middleton Street in South Nashville. Between Lindsley Avenue and Middleton Street, University Street formed the eastern border of the campus of Peabody Normal College. The street was named for the old University of Nashville that preceded the Peabody Normal College on the site.

US HIGHWAY 70 was built in 1926 as a national highway that originally ran from Beaufort, in eastern North Carolina, all the way to Holbrook, Arizona. It was called the "Broadway of America" because, before the interstates, it was one of the major east-west routes in the country. Locally, the highway crosses Nine-Mile Hill, which was named because of its distance from the city.

In the 1930s–40s, Hettie Ray's café and dance hall, on the top of Nine-Mile Hill, was a favorite hangout for Belle Meade teenagers. Frances Johnston Earthman went there on dates in the 1940s. For the fifty-cent minimum, she could spend the evening dancing to the nickelodeon and ordering soft drinks and potato chips. At the end of the evening, the boys would coast down Nine-Mile Hill to save gas. Hettie Ray's building burned in the 1950s.

Rand McNally's *Nashville Street Guide for 2006* still showed Harding Pike and US Highway 70 South as part of the Memphis-Bristol Highway and State Highway 1. *See Lebanon Pike.*

VALLEY BROOK ROAD, in Woodmont Estates, was built in 1937 as part of the subdivision of G. A. Puryear's farm that had earlier been part of Samuel Watkins' plantation. The Olmstead Brothers Company, an influential land design firm, designed the roads in Woodmont Estates so that the lots flowed naturally with the hills, valleys, and brooks. Charles Hawkins, city engineer, had suggested to Puryear that he and E. L. Hampton employ the firm to do this. *See Concrete* and *Woodmont Boulevards.*

VAN BUREN STREET was named for Martin Van Buren, the eighth president of the United States. It is located in north Nashville.

VANDERBILT AVENUE ran from Church Street south to Hillsboro Pike west of Boyd Avenue. Vanderbilt Avenue became part of Twenty-First Avenue South in 1904.

*US Highway 70 veers off to the right beyond this sign on Harding Road. The billboard encourages travellers headed toward Memphis to use US 70 instead of State Highway 100. Notice the Gerst Beer sign on the nightclub immediately behind the sign.*

SCOTT R. MERTIE COLLECTION

**VANDERBILT PLACE** extends from Twenty-Fifth Avenue North, in front of Memorial Gymnasium, north, passing Branscomb Quadrangle on the right, before crossing Twenty-Fourth Avenue North and ending at the entrance to the Sarratt Cinema. Another segment of Vanderbilt Place begins at Natchez Trace near Twenty-Eighth Avenue South and runs west to Thirty-Second Avenue South. The street was named for Commodore Cornelius Vanderbilt, who promised Bishop Holland McTyeire a total gift of no less than $500,000 to start Vanderbilt University in 1873. Before his death early in 1877, Commodore Vanderbilt had given the university a total of almost $1 million.

**VAUGHN PIKE** (later called Eastland Avenue) led to the Vaughn farm on the Cumberland River. It was named for the family who lived there from 1810 to 1909, when Hiram Vaughn sold the farm to Dr. and Mrs. Rufus E. Fort. In 1889, when Grantland Rice, the famous sportswriter, was eight years old, his family moved from his grandfather's house on Woodland Street to Vaughn Pike. There, Grantland grew up "with trees to climb and room to roam."[29] In the spring, he'd fly kites and play baseball in the open fields along the pike; in the summer, he'd swim in the Cumberland River; and, in the winter, he'd skate on Shelby Pond and sled down nearby hills. *See Eastland Avenue.*

**VAUGHN'S GAP ROAD** begins at Jocelyn Hollow Road and runs south to Highway 100. The road and Vaughn's Gap, a short distance southwest, were named for Johnson Vaughn, a prosperous farmer in the area.

**VAULX LANE,** in Berry Hill, runs from Ninth Avenue South to Gale Lane. It was named for Joseph Vaulx, president of the Tennessee Marine and Fire Company. He lived on Franklin Pike, three miles south of town.

**VAUXHALL PLACE** ran from Broad Street to Demonbreun, one block west of Spruce Street. It was named for the old Vauxhall Gardens, "a fashionable resort in the southern outskirts of the city said to have been modeled after the London resort of the same name." John Bell made his famous "Vauxhall Gardens Speech" there on May 23, 1835, and President Andrew Jackson was honored there on several occasions.[30] The gardens, established by Decker & Dyer in 1827, operated for more than a decade. The six-story Vauxhall Flats stood at the corner of Broad and Vauxhall in 1901. After Dr. George W. Price, principal for the Nashville College for Young Ladies, died, Vanderbilt University bought the three connected buildings. One was used for the dental school, while the other two were converted into apartments. All the other buildings on the street in 1900 were residences, some very handsome. Vauxhall Place became part of Ninth Avenue South in 1904. There is also a Vauxhall Drive in Bellevue. *See Ninth Avenue.*

**VILLA PLACE** runs from South Street up the long, gradual hill to Belmont Boulevard. In 1908, parade grounds were at Edgehill between Villa Place and Fifteenth Avenue South. That October, Ringling Brothers Circus held three performances there. In the 1950s–60s, there were a number of nice homes on Villa Place, including some that could be described as villas. The street was named by Adelicia Acklen's family.

**VINE HILL ROAD** runs north and south for three or four blocks between Bransford Avenue and Interstate 65 South. It carries the name of Vine Hill, the home of William Gerst, who owned the William Gerst Brewing Company for many years. In 1896, his beer won the gold ribbon at the Tennessee Centennial Exposition. Vine Hill was torn down in about 1940, to make room for temporary housing for defense workers. In 1952, the property was acquired by the City of Nashville for use as public housing, specifically 130 duplexes at 2108 Vine Hill Road.

VINE STREET took the name of Vine Street in Philadelphia. The name was appropriate because of the beautiful vines at the Felix Grundy home, Grundy Hill, one entrance to which was on Vine Street. Senator Douglas Henry Jr. pointed out to me that there is still a tiny remnant of the former Vine Street left. It is a block-long street in the triangle between Eighth Avenue South, Interstate 40, and Lafayette Street in South Nashville. When James K. Polk and his wife, Sarah, purchased Grundy Hill to make it their home after he finished his one term as president in 1849, they renamed the house Polk Place. *See Seventh Avenue.*

VOSSLAND DRIVE, in West Meade, was named for Ronald L. Voss, who was a partner in the syndicate that acquired 1,750 acres in West Meade in 1944. Voss personally purchased the West Meade mansion and fifty acres that year from the heirs of Supreme Court Justice Howell E. Jackson and his wife, Elizabeth Harding Jackson.

VOSSWOOD DRIVE, also named for Ronald L. Voss, is in West Meade. It runs between Brook Hollow Road and Davidson Road.

VULTEE BOULEVARD extends from Murfreesboro Pike to the Vultee plant opened in May 1941 by the Aviation Manufacturing Corporation of California to produce Vultee Vengeance bombers for use in World War II. Both the boulevard and the bombers were named for Gerald "Jerry" Vultee, vice president and chief engineer of AVCO's Vultee Aircraft Division.

WARNER PLACE, in Belle Meade, was subdivided between Jackson Boulevard and the old Belle Meade stone wall following the subdivision plat being filed in March 1914. Luke Lea, who developed the property, named Warner Place for his wife's parents, Mr. and Mrs. Percy Warner.

WATER STREET shows on Thomas Malloy's 1784 map of Nashville. It was given that name because it ran along the bluff of the Cumberland River, both north and south of the public square. The name was subsequently changed to Front Street and, in 1904, to First Avenue. *See First Avenue* and *Front Street.*

WAXHAW DRIVE, between Stewarts Ferry Pike and McCrory Creek, was named for the area along the North and South Carolina boundary where Andrew Jackson was born.

WEAVER ROAD, near the Nashville International Airport east of Murfreesboro Pike, was named for the family that lived on the pike. Mr. and Mrs. Dempsey Weaver lived at Kingsley in 1860, while their son, Thomas S. Weaver, built Sevenoaks in 1890.

WEDGEWOOD AVENUE was named for a famous race horse. Wedgewood was a champion trotter that was undefeated on the Grand Circuit in 1880, earning the title the "Iron Horse." Nashville Mayor May Overton purchased Wedgewood for $25,000 and brought him to Nashville in 1886. In 1974, Wedgewood Avenue ran from the fairgrounds to Eighth Avenue South. The street was later extended from Eighth Avenue South, initially to Fifteenth Avenue South, and then on to Twenty-First Avenue South.

WELLESLEY TRACE is located in Dudley Warner II's first cluster home development. In 1976, he acquired options to purchase the back yards of seven homeowners on the east side of Twenty-Second Avenue South. Dudley then exercised the options and built seventeen homes on the street that is between Glouster Square and Twenty-Second Avenue South. The development was completed in 1980. He named the street for Wellesley, Massachusetts, one of Boston's most elite suburbs.

WEST BROOKFIELD DRIVE, that goes from Belle Meade Boulevard northwest to Page Road, was advertized as part of the Highlands of Belle Meade, developed by the Belle Meade Land Company soon after the plat was recorded on August 21, 1928. Also included was Canterbury Drive and the west side of Belle Meade Boulevard between West Tyne and Page Road. In the mid-1930s, when Mr. and Mrs. Jesse E. Wills lived at today's 1201 Belle

Meade Boulevard, their mailing address was "Mr. and Mrs. J. E. Wills, Highlands of Belle Meade, Nashville, Tennessee."

WEST END AVENUE extended west to the city limits. In 1889, the McGavock and Mt. Vernon Horse Railroad Company acquired six electric streetcars that they ran out West End Avenue. The main entrance to the Tennessee Centennial Celebration was on West End. On opening day, May 1, 1897, people came to the centennial event on streetcars, in tallyhos, wagonettes, traps, and the railroad.

When the Nashville Golf and Country Club was built on Harding Pike beyond the city limits, a wagonette took golfers from the last streetcar stop on West End to the clubhouse in 1901. When the park was opened to the public in 1903, handsome homes lined West End from just west of Union Station to Vanderbilt on the south side, and to the park on the north side. In October that year, sixteen thousand people attended the opening performance of the Barnum and Bailey Circus, "the greatest show on earth," with one hundred acts, five hundred horses, and tents covering twelve acres on West End Avenue across from Centennial Park.

*This circa 1917 view of the entrance to Acklen Park from West End Avenue does not show Joseph A. Acklen's home, Acklen, which was on the top of the hill to the left, hidden by the trees.*
RIDLEY WILLS II COLLECTION

In 1906, the city limits were extended out West End to Mockingbird Road beyond the country club, making access to the club easier. In April of that year, the Richland Realty Company ran a full-page ad in the *Nashville Banner* showing a plat of lots on West End Avenue facing south and on Richland and Central Avenues, between Wilson Avenue on the west and the Tennessee Central Railroad track on the east.

For many years in the second half of the twentieth century, Candyland on West End was a favorite place to eat. Who could forget Uncle Billy serving up a big scoop of Candyland's chocolate ice cream covered with marshmallow sauce and thousands of pieces of chocolate sprinkles?

**WEST END CIRCLE**, in Acklen Park, was the centerpiece of West End Park (later named Acklen Park) when that exclusive subdivision was developed in 1915. On the crest of the hill west of West End Circle was Joseph H. Acklen's home, Acklen, that was destroyed by fire in 1961. The first map of West End Park was recorded on July 22, 1893.

**WESTLAWN DRIVE** was created when the Richland Realty Company subdivided eleven lots extending to Murphy Road in 1924. The street is south of Murphy Road, east of McCabe Golf Course.

**WESTMORELAND AVENUE** runs diagonally from Sharondale to Blair. Its inception came in 1922, when fifty choice residential lots were offered for sale in what was then called Westmoreland Place by George R. Gillespie Company, and W. W. Dillon and Company.

**WESTOVER DRIVE** was developed by Bransford Realty Company in 1915 as a portion of the Belle Meade Golf Links subdivision. A large segment of Westover bordering the Nashville Golf and Country Club was later renamed Harding Place. The section of Westover from today's Harding Place to Leake Avenue was redeveloped by the Country Club Land Company. The plat for this section was recorded on July 2, 1917.

**WESTVIEW AVENUE** extends from Tyne Boulevard on the south to Lynnwood Boulevard. In its center, the road rides the crest of a hill with a splendid view to the west. Paralleling the street for much of its length is the stone wall that marked the eastern edge of Belle Meade plantation. Earlier, a short portion of Westview was initially named Bonaire Street and then Highland Avenue. *See Bonaire Street.*

**WESTWOOD AVENUE** extends west from Hillsboro Pike to near Interstate 440. It may have been named for West Wood, a historic home on what would become the Franklin Pike, built in 1804 by Mr. Thomas Deaderick.

**WHARF AVENUE,** in 1898, ran from Fillmore Street south to Trimble Street in South Nashville. Its name came from its proximity to the lower wharf on the Cumberland River.

**WHELESS AVENUE** runs northeast from Dr. D. B. Todd Jr. Boulevard to Eleventh Avenue North. The street was named for J. F. Wheless, a real estate developer with the Waverly Land Company in the 1880s.

**WHISPERING HILLS DRIVE** is a continuation of Blackman Road. It goes southeast to McMurray Drive. Robert T. "Bob" Coleman and his father, Samuel F. Coleman, developed the street and named it for the hills in the vicinity that seemed to whisper in the wind.

**WHITE AVENUE** begins at Benton Avenue and goes south past Craighead Street in Waverly-Belmont. The street was named for John P. White, a real estate agent with the Waverly Land Company that was active in the 1880s.

**WHITE BRIDGE ROAD** was, before the turn of the century, called Whitworth's Lane, although most maps identified it only as a "county road." About 1912, the county and the N. C. & St. L. Railroad agreed to replace the dangerous wagon bridge over the railroad tracks and Richland Creek with a concrete girder bridge 512 feet long and 48 feet above the creek. Some months later, a sand-colored bridge was built, designed by Howard M. Jones, grandfather of Nashvillian Charles W. Cook Jr. To prevent weathering and to smooth its finish, a white cement coating was applied. The result was such a dazzling white finish that it hurt the eyes. The bridge was visible from beyond Belle Meade Boulevard to the west and from Dutchman's Curve toward town. From then on, the road has been called "White Bridge Road."

**WHITES CREEK PIKE** had its beginning as a turnpike that led from a bridge over the Cumberland River, through the community of Whites Creek, and northwest to the top of Paradise Ridge. There, it met dirt roads leading to Clarksville and Springfield. The turnpike, started in 1829, was the county's second oldest. Before, during, and after the Civil War, Paradise Ridge had a reputation for wildness. Men gathered there at country stores, exchanged gossip, drank whiskey, and fought chickens and each other. Murders were a relatively common occurrence.

**WHITLAND AVENUE**'s eastern terminus is at Bowling Avenue, across from Elmington Park. The street goes west before curving northwest into West End Avenue across from Mockingbird Lane. The street was named for the Whitland Real Estate Company, formed in 1910 by Dr. R. W. Grizzard, Charles Whitworth, and three others. The company purchased the land from Gertrude B. Bowling and subdivided the Whitland area. In the 1920s, the Fugitive Poets (a group of Nashville poets who drew national acclaim during the 1920s) met at Stanley Frank's home on Whitland.

**WHITSETT ROAD** runs east off of Nolensville Pike. It was named for James Whitsett, first pastor of the Mill Creek Baptist Church, established in 1797. For many years an old flat rock stood near the intersection of Nolensville Pike and Whitsett Road. The rock gave the Woodbine area its first name, "Flat Rock."

**WILBURN STREET** runs from Meridian Street to Lischey Avenue one block south of Cleveland Street. It was named for either Mr. Theophilus Wilburn Crutcher, who lived around the corner at 832 Lischey Avenue, or a member of his family. Mr. Crutcher's sister, Jennie (Mrs. J. A.) Green, lived on Crutcher Street early in the twentieth century. *See Crutcher Street* and *Lischey Avenue.*

**WILSON BOULEVARD** extends from Harding Pike to Oaklawn Avenue. Its northern terminus was, early in the twentieth century, at Wilson Switch, where the electric streetcar motorman had to switch the trolley for the return trip to town. Wilson Boulevard was named for Mr. and Mrs. B. F. Wilson, whose beautiful home, Wilmor Manor, stood across Harding Pike, until it burned in 1916. Mr. Wilson was a capitalist and director of the First Savings Bank and Trust Company.

**WILSONIA AVENUE**, in Hillwood, parallels Hillwood Boulevard and runs from Post Road to Hickory Valley Road. The street was named by H. G. Hill Jr. for his mother, Mamie Wilson Hill.

**WINDING WAY DRIVE**, in Inglewood, was part of the Jackson Park subdivision incorporated in 1930 to create the Belle Meade of East Nashville. The subdivision extended from Gallatin Pike to Brush Hill Road, and had oversized lots and sidewalks. Clifton Beverly Briley (1914–) lived on Winding Way when he was elected the first mayor of the Metropolitan Government of Nashville and Davidson County in 1963.

**WINDSOR DRIVE** runs from Harding Place, in front of Harding Academy, to Westover Drive in what was, in 1917, called the Belle Meade Golf Links subdivision. The meandering curves in the subdivision suggest that Bransford employed landscape designer Ossian Cole Simonds (1855–1931) to assist in the aesthetically pleasing design. The subdivision had three private parks for the exclusive use of the homeowners. The small parks featured a grid pattern of paths.

**WOODLAND STREET** parallels Main Street in East Nashville. Both start at bridges over the Cumberland River and run east, terminating at Shelby Park. Woodland Street was cut through in the late 1850s when Dr. John Shelby's home, Woodland, between Second and Third Streets, was torn down and the land subdivided. Woodland Street runs through the location of his house. Late in the nineteenth century, East Nashville was one of the city's most attractive residential areas, with towering hardwood trees and handsome homes.

When he was a little boy in the 1880s, Grantland Rice, the nationally acclaimed sportswriter, lived in his grandfather's spacious, high-ceilinged house at 614 Woodland Street for five years. Mr. Henry Grantland's home was one mile from the public square, easily accessible by the Nashville and Edgefield Street Railroad Company's line.

The historic East Nashville fire of March 22, 1916, destroyed most of the buildings in its path, including the Woodland Street Christian Church and Woodland Street Presbyterian Church. At the height of the fire, fifteen expensive homes on Woodland Street were burning simultaneously.

The Woodland Street Theater opened in 1920. It advertised itself as "Nashville's Ace Suburban Theater, Complete Change of Programs Three Times A Week."[31]

**WOODLAWN DRIVE** runs from Harding Pike to Hillsboro Pike. It was named for Woodlawn, the home built by Capt. John Nichols in 1823, on what would become Richland Turnpike. That same year, Willoughby Williams married Nichols's daughter, Nancy. Soon, he took charge of his father-in-law's affairs and, in time, acquired ownership of the house and property. Williams, a colonel in the state militia and sheriff of Davidson County, also had a stud named Woodlawn. At the eastern end of Woodlawn Drive, Belair, a home built by Matthew Allen in about 1884, still stands facing south. Earlier, the Queen Anne–style home stood across the street on a stretch earlier called Belair. In 1900, the hill at the intersection of Hillsboro Pike and Woodlawn Drive was called Allen's Hill for Matthew Allen. *See Kenner Avenue.*

**WOODMONT BOULEVARD** began as Concrete Boulevard when it was built as a private road by W. H. Armstead, E. L. Hampton, and G. A. Puryear in 1914. The road was renamed Woodmont boulevard in 1916 for Puryear's home, Woodmont, on the west side of Hillsboro Pike, slightly south of the boulevard. Because it was in the country, was relatively smooth, and had little traffic, Woodmont was a favorite place to teach teenagers to drive. In the mid-1930s, the road was repaved and extended to Franklin Pike. *See Concrete Boulevard.*

**WORTHAM AVENUE** begins at Sterling Avenue and runs north to Woodlawn Drive. It was part of the Stokes Tract development by E. L. Hampton in 1937. Hampton named the street for his son-in-law, Eban Wortham, who married his daughter, Melinda Hampton Wortham. Hampton's lots were sold in an area bounded by Golf Club Lane on the south and Compton Road on the northwest. At the time, Wortham was called Midland Avenue.

**WYOMING AVENUE** is one of twenty streets in West Nashville named for states. In about 1800, Hewitt Childress built a plantation house at what is now the corner of Wyoming and Fifty-First Avenues. His home faced Richland Creek and an early road to Bosley Springs. *See California Avenue.*

**YMCA WAY** was named in 2010 to recognize the significance of the YMCA of Middle Tennessee at 1000 Church Street on the corner of what had been McLemore Street. YMCA Way extends from Charlotte Avenue to Church Street just as McLemore did.

# NOTES

1. "What's In A Name," *The Daily American*, February 8, 1886.
2. Ibid.
3. "Nashville Club Women Ask Restoration of Street Names," *Nashville Banner*, March 13, 1909.
4. "Street Names Bill Defeated," *The Nashville American*, April 23, 1909.
5. Wilbur Foster Creighton, *Life Story of Robert Thomas Creighton* (Nashville: privately published, 1967), 32.
6. Wikipedia, American Baptist College; conversation, author with Dr. Forrest E. Harris Sr., president, American Baptist College, October 6, 2011.
7. George Zepp, "Buford College Sought Only Women of Promise," *The Tennessean*, June 26, 2002.
8. "Assemblymen to the Rescue," *The Nashville American*, April 23, 1909.
9. Creighton, *Life Story of Robert Thomas Creighton*, 30.
10. Nashville newspaper, 1915.

11. Mary Bray Wheeler and Genon Hickerson Neblett, *Chosen Exile: The Life and Times of Septima Sexta Middleton Rutledge, American Cultural Pioneer* (Nashville: Rutledge Hill Press, 1980), 74.

12. Paul H. Beasley, *A Directory of Nashville and Davidson County Historical Markers* (Metropolitan Nashville Retired Teachers Association, 1977), 31.

13. Article by John Wesley Gaines, Nashville newspaper, March 1908.

14. North Carolina Territorial Legislature Act passed April 5, 1796. John E. Windrow, ed., *Peabody and Alfred Leland Crabb* (Nashville: Williams Press, 1977), 29.

15. "Inglewood Auction," *The Nashville American*, May 23, 1909.

16. "A Coming American Champion," *Nashville American*, October 17, 1898.

17. Ken Roberts Jr., "One For the Road: Stories of Nashville's Hard-drinking Nightlife," *Nashville Scene*, June 13, 1996.

18. Nashville newspaper, 1925.

19. E. Michael Fleenor, *Images of America: East Nashville* (Charleston, SC: Arcadia Publishing, 1998), 19.

20. Mrs. James E. Caldwell, "Melrose," *Beautiful and Historical Homes In and Near Nashville, Tennessee* (Nashville: Brandon Printing Co., 1913), unpaged.

21. John Lawrence Connelly, *North Nashville and Germantown* (Nashville: Ambrose Printing Co., 1982), 57.

22. Conversation, author with Wentworth Caldwell Jr., October 4, 2011.

23. Article on Old Hickory Boulevard, *Nashville Tennessean*, July 1936.

24. H. W. Crew, *History of Nashville, Tennessee* (Nashville: Publishing House of the Methodist Episcopal Church, South, 1890), 322.

25. Jack Norman Sr., "Turnpike Companies Operated Area Roads," Nashville newspaper, date unknown.

26. Inscription on "Greetings from Villa Crest Hotel and Cottages, Ridgetop, Tenn." postcard (Ridley Wills II Collection).

27. Leland R. Johnson, *The Parks of Nashville: A History of the Board of Parks and Recreation* (Metropolitan Nashville and Davidson County Board of Parks and Recreation, 1986), 77.

28. William Waller, *Nashville in the 1890s* (Nashville: Vanderbilt University Press, 1970), 198-99.

29. Charles Fountain, *Sportswriter: The Life and Times of Grantland Rice* (Oxford: Oxford University Press, 1993), 37.

30. Jospeh Howard Parks, *John Bell of Tennessee* (Baton Rouge: Louisiana State University Press, 1950), 80, 100.

31. Fleenor, *Images of America: East Nashville*, 100.